BRAIN-
BUSTING
LATERAL
THINKING
PUZZLES

Official Mensa
Puzzle Book

BRAIN-
BUSTING
LATERAL
THINKING
PUZZLES

PAUL SLOANE & DES MACHALE

Illustrated by Myron Miller

STERLING PUBLISHING CO., INC.
NEW YORK

Mensa and the distinctive table logo are trademarks of
American Mensa, Ltd. (in the U.S.),
British Mensa, Ltd. (in the U.K.),
Australian Mensa, Inc. (in Australia),
and Mensa International Limited (in other countries)
and are used by permission.

Library of Congress Cataloging-in-Publication Data Available

6   8   10   9   7   5

Published in 2004 by Sterling Publishing Co., Inc.
387 Park Avenue South, New York, NY 10016
This book is comprised of material from *Improve Your Lateral Thinking*
by Paul Sloane and Des MacHale © 1998 by Paul Sloane and Des
MacHale and *Ingenious Lateral Thinking Puzzles* by Paul Sloane and
Des MacHale © 1998 by Paul Sloane and Des MacHale
Distributed in Canada by Sterling Publishing
℅ Canadian Manda Group, 165 Dufferin Street
Toronto, Ontario, Canada M6K 3H6
Distributed in Great Britain by Chrysalis Books Group PLC
The Chrysalis Building, Bramley Road, London, W10 6SP, England
Distributed in Australia by Capricorn Link (Australia) Pty. Ltd.
P.O. Box 704, Windsor, NSW 2756, Australia

Sterling ISBN 1-4027-1249-9

For information about custom editions, special sales, premium and
corporate purchases, please contact Sterling Special Sales
Department at 800-805-5489 or specialsales@sterlingpub.com.

ACKNOWLEDGMENTS

This book is dedicated to Woody Allen, Clarence Birdseye, Richard Branson, Edward de Bono, George Boole, Filippo Brunelleschi, Nicolaus Copernicus, Thomas Edison, Albert Einstein, Dick Fosbury, Galieli Galileo, Guglielmo Marconi, Groucho Marx, Sir Thomas More, Sir Isaac Newton, Tom Peters, Leonardo da Vinci, Oscar Wilde, Steven Wright, Orville and Wilbur Wright, and lateral thinkers everywhere.

CONTENTS

INSTRUCTIONS

1. Grab some other people. It's better to do these puzzles in a group of two or more than to try and solve them individually. Typically, they contain insufficient information for you to deduce the solution. You need to ask questions in order to gather more information before you can formulate solutions.
2. Start with the "Warm-Up Puzzles." They are a little easier.
3. One person acts as quizmaster. He or she reads the puzzle out loud and reads the solution silently.
4. The people trying to solve the puzzle ask questions in order to gather information, check assumptions, and test possible solutions.
5. The quizmaster can answer in one of four ways: "Yes," "No," "Irrelevant," or "Please rephrase the question."
6. If the solvers get stuck, the quizmaster can offer one or more of the clues given in the "Clues" section.
7. The aim is to arrive at the solution given in the "Answers" section, not simply to find a situation that satisfies the initial conditions. If you want to award points for good alternatives, you can, but the answer given is the true goal.
8. The person who solves the puzzle gets the kudos, recognition, and prestige. Credit should also be given to those who ask the key lateral questions.
9. Strategy tip: Test your assumptions, and ask broad questions that establish general conditions, motives, and actions. Don't narrow in on specific solutions until you have first established the broad parameters of what's going on.
10. When you get stuck, attack the problem from a new direction—think laterally! Have fun!

INTRODUCTION

When the Wright brothers set out to build a flying machine, many intelligent people assured them that their project was a fool's errand. Everybody knew that a machine that was heavier than air could not fly. When Marconi tried to transmit a radio signal from England to Canada, the experts scoffed at the idea of sending radio waves around the curved surface of the Earth. But Marconi succeeded. When Copernicus and then Galileo proposed that the Sun, not the Earth, was the center of the known universe, they were condemned as dangerous heretics. Yet each of these people changed the world by defying conventional thinking and by coming up with a radically new and better solution to an existing problem.

This is the core of lateral thinking—solving problems by the use of creative new approaches. The skills of lateral thinking can be honed by attempting to unravel and piece together what happened in unfamiliar situations, such as the puzzles in this book. This can be great fun and very challenging. Coming up with the answers involves asking the right questions, to ascertain what is really going on in the situation, and then figuring out the answer—not just any possible answer, but the answer given.

Each puzzle has been rated, ranging from 2 (easy) to 4 (very difficult). The rating can be used to score how good you are at solving lateral thinking puzzles. Do the puzzles with a friend and take turns as puzzle setter and solver. The solver can ask questions about the puzzle. The puzzle setter should answer the question with either "yes," "no," or "irrelevant." If the solver solves the puzzle within twenty minutes, then he or she scores the puzzle rating: 2, 3, or 4. If the solver gets stuck, then the puzzle setter can give the solver a clue from the clues section, but each clue

11

costs a point. (Only one clue is provided for easy puzzles.) So, if you need two clues to help solve a puzzle with a 4 rating, you score two points. If you can score fifteen points or more from a sequence of ten puzzles, you are doing well. You will see your scores improve as you progress at asking questions and thinking of lateral solutions.

The puzzles are designed to be fun. As you do them, your skills in checking assumptions, questioning, deduction, using your imagination, and putting the pieces together should all improve. You can apply these same techniques to aid you in problem solving in everyday life. Who knows? You could conceive a brilliant idea, make a breakthrough, and confound the doubters just like the Wright brothers did!

THE PUZZLES

Warm-Up Puzzles

Angry Response

A man called his wife from the office to say that he would be home at around eight o'clock. He got in at two minutes past eight. His wife was extremely angry at his late arrival. Why?

Clues: 99/Answer: 145.

Picture Purchase

An art expert went to a sale and bought a picture he knew to be worthless. Why?

Clues: 124/Answer: 165.

Alone in a Boat

Why are two little animals alone in a little boat in the middle of the ocean?

Clues: 99/Answer: 144.

Strangulation

A famous dancer was found strangled. The police did not suspect murder. Why not?

Clues: 134/Answer: 173.

Complete Garbage

The garbage was emptied out of the cans and a man died. How?

Clues: 106/Answer: 150.

Golf Bag

During a golf competition, Paul's ball ended up in a bunker inside a little brown paper bag that had blown onto the course. He was told that he must either play the ball in the bag or take the ball out of the bag and incur a one stroke penalty. What did he do?

Clues: 113/Answer: 157.

Flipping Pages

Yesterday, I went through a book, which I had already read, in a peculiar manner. After I finished a page, I flipped to the next page, then rotated the book 180 degrees. After that page, I rotated the book 180 degrees and then flipped to the next page, rotated the book 180 degrees again, and continued in this fashion until I was done with the whole book. What was going on?

Clues: 111/Answer: 155.

Leadfoot and Gumshoe

A woman is stopped for speeding. The police officer gives her a warning, but the woman insists that she be given a ticket and a fine, which she promptly pays. Why did she want the ticket and fine?

Clues: 117/Answer: 160.

Man in Tights

A man wearing tights is lying unconscious in a field. Next to him is a rock. What happened?

Clues: 118/Answer: 160.

Straight Ahead

When the Eisenhower Interstate Highway System was built, it was specified that one mile in every five must be absolutely straight. Why?

Clues: 134/Answer: 173.

Motion Not Passed

A referendum motion was not passed. If more people had voted against it, however, it would have passed. How come?

Clues: 120/Answer: 162.

Russian Racer

At the height of the Cold War, a U.S. racing car easily beat a Russian car in a two-car race. How did the Russian newspapers truthfully report this in order to make it look as though the Russian car had outdone the American car?

Clues: 129/Answer: 169.

Waterless Rivers

Now for a riddle: What has rivers but no water, cities but no buildings, and forests but no trees?

Clues: 138/Answer: 177.

The Test

The teacher gave Ben and Jerry a written test. Ben read the test, then folded his arms and answered none of the questions. Jerry carefully wrote out good answers to the questions. When the time was up, Ben handed in a blank sheet of paper while Jerry handed in his work. The teacher gave Ben an A and Jerry a C. Why?

Clues: 135/Answer: 174.

Statue of an Insect

Why is there a commemorative statue of an insect in a little town in the state of Alabama?

Clues: 133/Answer: 172.

Fired for Joining Mensa

Mensa is a club for clever people. Anne's employer has no anti-Mensa feeling, but has made it clear to her that if she ever joins Mensa she will lose her job. How come?

Clues: 111/Answer: 154.

Six-Foot Drop

A man standing on solid concrete dropped a tomato six feet, but it did not break or bruise. How come?

Clues: 131/Answer: 171.

Seven Bells

A little shop in New York is called The Seven Bells, yet it has eight bells hanging outside. Why?

Clues: 130/Answer: 170.

Reentry

What took nineteen years to get into itself?

Clues: 127/Answer: 168.

Assault and Battery

John is guilty of no crime, but he is surrounded by professional people, one of whom hits him until he cries. Why?

Clues: 100/Answer: 145.

Up in the Air

One hundred feet up in the air, it lies with its back on the ground. What is it?

Clues: 137/Answer: 177.

Clean Shaven

Why did Alexander the Great order all his men to shave?

Clues: 106/Answer: 150.

Adolf Hitler

During the war, a British soldier had Adolf Hitler clearly in the sights of his gun. Why didn't he fire?

Clues: 98/Answer: 144.

Winning Numbers

I have on a piece of paper the winning numbers in next week's lotto jackpot. I am an avid gambler, yet I feel I have very little chance of winning. Why?

Clues: 139/Answer: 178.

Fair Fight

A boxer left the ring after winning the world championship. His trainer took all the money and he never got a cent. Why not?

Clues: 110/Answer: 153.

Unknown Recognition

I saw a man I had never seen before, but I immediately knew who he was. He was not famous and had never been described to me. He was not unusual nor doing anything unusual. How did I recognize him?

Clues: 137/Answer: 176.

Riddle of the Sphinx

The Sphinx asked this famous riddle: What is it that goes on four legs in the morning, two legs in the afternoon, and three legs in the evening?

Clues: 128/Answer: 168.

Unclimbed

Why has no one climbed the largest known extinct volcano?

Clues: 137/Answer: 176.

Talking to Herself

A woman is talking sadly. Nobody can understand her, but a man is filming her intently. Why?

Clues: 135/Answer: 174.

Workout Puzzles

The Unlucky Bed

A certain bed in a certain hospital acquires the reputation of being unlucky. Whichever patient is assigned to this bed seems to die there on a Friday evening. A watch is kept by camera and the reason is discovered. What is it?

Clues: 137/Answer: 176.

Missing Items

What two items does a boy have at ten years of age that he did not have when he was one year old?

Clues: 119/Answer: 161.

Once Too Often

If you do it once, it's good. If you do it twice on the same day, though, it's a serious crime. What is it?

Clues: 122/Answer: 164.

Noteworthy

A woman took a picture of a U.S. president to her bank. As a result a criminal was arrested. How?

Clues: 122/Answer: 163.

Rejected Shoes

A man bought a pair of shoes that were in good condition and that fit him well. He liked the style and they looked good. However, after he had worn them for one day he took them back to the shop and asked for a refund. Why?

Clues: 127/Answer: 168.

Slow Drive

Why does a man drive his car on a long journey at a steady fifteen miles per hour? The speed limit is well above that and his car is in full working order and capable of high speeds.

Clues: 131/Answer: 171.

Weak Case

The police charged a man with a crime. They had a weak case against him. He posted his bail. The police then had a strong case against him. Why?

Clues: 139/Answer: 177.

The Man Who Got Water

A man parked his car on the road, walked into a building, returned with some water, and poured the water onto the sidewalk. Why?

Clues: 118/Answer: 161.

The Writer

A man who was paralyzed in his arms, legs, and mouth, and unable to speak a word, wrote a best-selling book. How?

Clues: 140/Answer: 179.

Chimney Problem

An industrial archaeologist was examining an abandoned factory in a remote place with no one in sight or within earshot. He climbed to the top of an old 100-foot chimney by means of a rusty old ladder attached to the outside of the chimney. When he got to the top, the ladder fell away, leaving him stranded. How did he get down?

Clues: 105/Answer: 150.

Happy Birthday

A man went into his local shopping center. A woman whom he had never met before wished him a happy birthday. How did she know it was his birthday?

Clues: 114/Answer: 157.

Acidic Action

A murderer killed his wife and dissolved her body completely in a bath of acid. What piece of evidence caused him to be caught?

Clues: 98/Answer: 144.

November 11

A large mail order company performed an analysis of its customers. It was surprised to learn that an unusually large number were born on November 11. How could this be?

Clues: 122/Answer: 164.

Garbage Nosiness

One morning last week I peered into my neighbor's garbage can and then drove to work feeling annoyed. One morning this week I peered into my other neighbor's garbage can and then drove off feeling even more annoyed. Why?

Clues: 112/Answer: 155.

Well-Meaning

How did an animal rights activist who had good intentions cause the death of the living creatures she was trying to save?

Clues: 139/Answer: 177.

Shooting a Dead Man

A policeman shot a dead man. He was not acting illegally. Why did he do it?

Clues: 131/Answer: 170.

Bottled Up

A cleaning woman asked the man she worked for if she could take home his empty bottles. When she got home, she threw them out. Why did she do this?

Clues: 102/Answer: 147.

Alex Ferguson

In the early 1990s, Alex Ferguson was the coach of Manchester United, the most successful professional soccer team in England at that time. Previously he had been a very successful manager in Scotland. He would be a very successful manager of a soccer team anywhere in the world, except Singapore. Why is that?

Clues: 99/Answer: 144.

Don't Get Up

A woman is reading a newspaper alone. She hears the phone ring in the room next to the one she is in. Although she knows that the call is probably important, she does not bother to answer it. Why not?

Clues: 108/Answer: 152.

Misunderstood

Part of the police manual gives instructions in a language that none of the policemen speaks. Why?

Clues: 119/Answer: 162.

Scuba Do

Why was a man driving down the street wearing a scuba face mask?

Clues: 129/Answer: 169.

WALLY Test I

From the World Association of Learning, Laughter, and Youth (WALLY) comes the WALLY Test! It is a set of quick-fire questions. They may look easy, but be warned—they are designed to trick you. Write down your answers on a piece of paper and then see how many you got right. The time limit is three minutes.

1. What is the last thing you take off before going to bed at night?
2. What gets longer when it is cut at both ends?
3. What was the first name of King George VI of England?
4. What do you call a fly without wings?
5. How many squares are there on a standard chess-board?
6. How many seconds are there in a year?
7. A man throws a ball three feet, it stops, and then returns to his hand without touching anything. How come?
8. What was the largest island in the world before Australia was discovered?
9. Why can a policeman never open the door in his pajamas?
10. If five dogs kill five rats in five minutes, how long does it take fifteen dogs to kill fifteen rats?

Answers on page 179-180.

Strenuous Puzzles

One Mile

If you go to your atlas and look at the western edge of the state of South Dakota where it borders Montana, you will see a straight line with a kink of about one mile. Everywhere else the border is a straight line. The kink does not benefit any local landowner and no other states are involved. Why is the kink there?

Clues: 123/Answer: 164.

The Unbroken Arm

Why did a perfectly healthy young girl put a full plaster cast on her arm when it was not injured in any way?

Clues: 136/Answer: 176.

The Shoplifter

A shoplifter starts stealing small items and over a period of time steals larger and larger items, but then suddenly stops altogether. What is going on?

Clues: 130/Answer: 171.

Getting Away with Murder

A man shot his wife dead. She was not threatening him or anyone else. He then gave himself up to the police. They released him. Why?

Clues: 113/Answer: 156.

Exceptional Gratitude

Why did Bill thank Ted for some eggs that Bill had never received and that Ted had never given?

Clues: 109/Answer: 153.

Dali's Brother

Some time after Salvador Dali's death, his younger brother became famous as (believe it or not) a surrealist painter. This younger brother had great international success and the word "genius" was used to describe him. His name was Dali and he did not change it. Yet today, the world remembers only one Dali and few people even know that he had a brother. Why is this?

Clues: 107/Answer: 151.

Bare Bones

During an examination, a medical student is handed a human femur (thigh bone). The examiner asks the student, "How many of these do you have?"

The student replies, "Five."

"Wrong," says the examiner, "You have two femurs."

But the student was right. How come?

Clues: 101/Answer: 146.

Two Clocks

A man was given two clocks by his wife as a Christmas present. He did not collect clocks and they already had plenty of clocks in the house. However, he was very pleased to receive them. Why?

Clues: 137/Answer: 175.

The Power of Tourism

In a certain place the local authorities, in order to increase tourism, have made the price of electricity higher. Why?

Clues: 126/Answer: 166.

Wiped Out

A woman got a job with a large company. After her first day's work she returned home utterly exhausted because of a misunderstanding. What had happened?

Clues: 140/Answer: 178.

88 Too Big

A man died because his number was 88 too big. How come?

Clues: 109/Answer: 153.

Invisible

What can you stand in front of in broad daylight and not see, even if you have perfect eyesight?

Clues: 116/Answer: 159.

The Auction

A man went to an auction to bid for something he wanted. He expected to pay about $100 for it, but ended up paying $500. There was no minimum price and no one bid against him. What happened?

Clues: 100/Answer: 145.

Poor Investment

Why did a company spend millions of dollars trying to find something that costs only a few thousand dollars?

Clues: 125/Answer: 166.

Nonexistent Actors

Why did the credits of a well-known movie list the names of four nonexistent actors?

Clues: 121/Answer: 163.

Machine Forge

A man builds a machine into which he feeds colored paper. Out of the other side come perfect $100 bills. Experts cannot tell them from real ones. How does he do it and why does he sell the machine?

Clues: 118/Answer: 160.

Spraying the Grass

The groundskeeper at a sports complex watered the grass every evening when the sun was setting. The grass grew fine. Before a major event, though, he sprayed the grass during the midday heat. Why?

Clues: 133/Answer: 172.

Wonder Horse

A horse that had lost every one of its previous races was entered in a horse race and came in first ahead of a top-class field. No drugs were used, and if the jockey had not confessed, then nobody would have known. What happened?

Clues: 141/Answer: 178.

Adrift in the Ocean

Two men are in a boat drifting in the Atlantic Ocean a hundred miles from the nearest land. They have no drinking water onboard, no radio, and they have no contact with any other boats or people. Yet they survive for a long time. How?

Clues: 98/Answer: 144.

Promotion

John is a young man working for a big company. He is lazy, poorly motivated, and inefficient. Yet he is the first person in his department to be promoted. Why?

Clues: 126/Answer: 167.

Barren Patch

A farmer has a patch of ground in the middle of one of his most fertile fields on which nothing will grow. Why not?

Clues: 101/Answer: 146.

Job Description

Two men were sitting in a crowded restaurant. A woman who was a total stranger to both of them walked in and told them her job. She said nothing more and they said nothing. What was going on?

Clues: 116/Answer: 159.

No More Bore

A notorious bore once called on Winston Churchill, who sent his butler to the door to say that Churchill was not at home. What suggestion did Churchill make to the butler to convince the caller that he really was not at home?

Clues: 121/Answer: 162.

Shaking a Fist

A policeman stopped a man for dangerous driving. As the policeman walked toward the car, the man rolled down the window and waved his fist at the policeman. Later, he thanked the policeman for saving his life. Why?

Clues: 130/Answer: 170.

Burnt Wood

Over the past 100 years many men have dedicated significant portions of their lives to the quest for some burnt wood. Although they have sometimes been successful, the burnt wood has never moved. What is it?

Clues: 103/Answer: 148.

The Wrong Ball

A golfer drove his ball out of sight over a hill. When he got there, he saw a ball that was the same make as his own and identical to it in every way. But he knew immediately that it was not his ball. How come?

Clues: 140/Answer: 179.

Window Pain

A builder builds a house that has a square window. It is two feet high and two feet wide. It is not covered by anything. The person for whom the house is being built decides that the window does not give enough light. He tells the builder to change the window so that it gives twice the amount of light. It must be in the same wall, and it must be a square window that is two feet high and two feet wide. How does the builder accomplish this task?

Clues: 139/Answer: 178.

Gas Attack

A man was sentenced to ten years' imprisonment with hard labor because he had kept the gas mask that the army had issued him. Why?

Clues: 112/Answer: 155-56.

WALLY Test II

Time for another WALLY Test. The questions may look easy, but be warned—they're designed to trip you up. Write down your answers on a piece of paper and then see how many you got right. The time limit is three minutes.

1. Rearrange these letters to make one new word: NEW NEW DOOR.
2. What do you find in seconds, minutes, and centuries, but not in days, years, or decades?
3. Which is correct: "Seven eights are 54" or "Seven eights is 54"?
4. Three men in a boat each had a cigarette, but they had no match, fire, or lighter. How did they light the cigarettes?
5. A clock strikes six o'clock in five seconds. How long does it take to strike noon or midnight?
6. What was the U.S. president's name in 1984?
7. Who won an Oscar for Best Actor and an Olympic gold medal for sprinting?
8. If two men can dig two holes in two days, how long does it take one man to dig half a hole?
9. An eighty-year-old prisoner was kept inside a high security prison with all the doors locked. He broke out. How?
10. If the post office clerk refused to stick a $4 stamp on your package, would you stick it on yourself?

Answers on page 180.

Super-Strenuous Puzzles

Bald Facts

A woman fell in love and, as a result, lost all her hair. Why?

Clues: 101/Answer: 146.

Fingerprint Evidence

The mass murderer Ted Bundy was very careful never to leave any fingerprints at the scene of any of his crimes, and he never did. Yet fingerprint evidence helped to incriminate him. How come?

Clues: 110/Answer: 154.

Hosing Down

Because it was raining, the firemen hosed down the road. Why?

Clues: 115/Answer: 158.

Pentagon Puzzle

The headquarters of the U.S. defense operations is the Pentagon in Arlington, Virginia. Why does it have twice as many bathrooms as it needs?

Clues: 124/Answer: 165.

Fill Her Up!

....

A woman bought her husband a beautiful new sports car as a present. When he first saw it, he filled it with wet cement and completely ruined it. Why?

Clues: 110/Answer: 154.

Three Spirals

....

A woman was pleased when she received three spirals instead of the usual two. When it was discovered that she had received three spirals, she was arrested. Why?

Clues: 135/Answer: 174-175.

You Can't Be Too Careful

....

Millions of people buy a particular medicine. The disease for which the medicine is effective is one that these people have virtually no chance of catching. What do they buy?

Clues: 141/Answer: 179.

Nonconventional

....

In a convent, the novice nuns at the dinner table are not allowed to ask for anything such as the salt from the other end of the table. This is because they should be so aware of one another's needs that they should not need to ask. How do they get around this prohibition?

Clues: 121/Answer: 163.

Replacing the Leaves

During fall, a little girl was in her backyard trying to stick the fallen leaves back onto the trees with glue. Why?

Clues: 127/Answer: 168.

Secret Assignment

The famous physicist Ulam one day noticed that several of his best graduate students had disappeared from his university. They had in fact gone to Los Alamos to take part in the top-secret preparations for the first atomic bomb. They were sworn to secrecy. How did Ulam find out where they had gone?

Clues: 129/Answer: 169.

The Ransom Note

A kidnapper sent a ransom note. He prepared it carefully and ensured that it contained no fingerprints. Yet it was used to prove his guilt. How?

Clues: 126/Answer: 167.

Debugging

How were insects once used in the diagnosis of a serious disease?

Clues: 108/Answer: 152.

Biography

An author died because he wrote a biography. How did he die?

Clues: 101/Answer: 146.

Ancient Antics

We generally consider ourselves to be a lot smarter and better educated than the people who lived in the prehistoric periods of the Stone Age, Iron Age, and Bronze Age. But what was it that men and women did in those times that no man or woman has managed to achieve for the last 4,000 years?

Clues: 99/Answer: 145.

Cartoon Character

What cartoon character owes his existence to a misprint in a scientific journal?

Clues: 105/Answer: 149.

The Carpet Seller

I bought a beautiful plain carpet measuring nine feet by sixteen feet from the carpet seller. When I got home I realized that my room was actually twelve feet by twelve feet. I returned to the carpet seller, who assured me that I could now exactly fit my room, provided I made just one cut to the original piece. Can you figure out how to do it?

Clues: 105/Answer: 149.

No Response

A man often answered questions in the course of his work. One day a stranger asked him a perfectly reasonable question that he refused to answer. Why?

Clues: 121/Answer: 163.

Walking Backward

A man walked backward from the front door of his house to his kitchen. Someone rang the doorbell and the man ran quickly out of his back door. Why?

Clues: 139/Answer: 177.

Free Lunch

A man in a restaurant used two forks and one knife. He did not pay for his lunch. What was happening?

Clues: 112/Answer: 155.

Right Off

A man comes out of his house to find that his new car is damaged beyond repair after he has paid for it, but before he has had time to insure it. However, he is absolutely delighted at what has happened. Why?

Clues: 128/Answer: 168.

Business Rivalry

Cain and Abel are business rivals. Cain cuts his price, and Abel then undercuts him. Cain then cuts his price even lower than Abel. Abel slashes his price to a ridiculous level and gets all the business, forcing Cain out of the market. But Cain has the last laugh. Why?

Clues: 104/Answer: 149.

Full Refund

A young couple went to a theater to watch a movie. After fifteen minutes they decided to leave. They had had a perfectly good view of the movie, which was running in perfect order. The cashier gave them a full refund. Why?

Clues: 112/Answer: 155.

A Day at the Races

A man was returning from a day at the races where he had made a lot of money. He was speeding in his car and was stopped by the police. The policeman took down all his details, but the man was never prosecuted nor suffered any penalty. Why not?

Clues: 107/Answer: 151.

Pass Protection

In the city where I live, commuters on the mass transit system can use monthly passes or single tokens. Today, I saw long lines of commuters waiting to buy passes and tokens. Those people with passes or tokens were able to bypass the lines. However, even though I had neither a pass nor a token, I was also able to walk right up to the turnstiles and pass through. How come?

Clues: 123/Answer: 165.

Easy Puzzles

Recovery *2 points*

A truck driver called in to his office to report that his truck had broken down. A tow truck was sent out to tow back the disabled truck. When they arrived, the truck that had broken down was towing the tow truck. Why?

Clue: 127/Answer: 167.

Man Overboard

2 points

A man holidaying abroad was alone on his yacht when he fell off into deep water. He was a nonswimmer and was not wearing anything to help keep him afloat. He was rescued half an hour later. Why didn't he drown?

Clue: 118/Answer: 160.

High Blood Pressure

2 points

During a medical examination, Gerald's blood pressure is found to be three times that of a normal healthy person. Yet neither Gerald nor his doctor is particularly worried about this. Why?

Clue: 114/Answer: 158.

The Great Wall

2 points

An American, who had never been to any country other than the United States, was standing one day on solid ground when he saw the Great Wall of China with his own eyes. How come?

Clue: 114/Answer: 157.

Poor Delivery

2 points

A Denver company ordered some goods from a European supplier. The American firm was very precise in stating the dates on which it wanted the deliveries to occur.

However, the European company, which generally had a high reputation for dependability, missed every delivery date by at least one month. Some shipments were very early and others were very late. Why?

Clue: 125/Answer: 166.

The Pilot's Son   *2 points*
··

A man and his son were traveling on a scheduled flight across the Atlantic. The man asked the flight attendant if his son could have a look inside the cockpit. The boy was allowed to do this and the pilot gladly explained about the plane and its controls. After the boy left, the pilot turned to the copilot and said to him, "That was my son." How could that be?

Clue: 124/Answer: 165.

Hole in One   *2 points*
··

A golfer had dreamed all her life of hitting her tee shot straight into the hole. However, one day she did this and was not at all pleased. Why not?

Clue: 115/Answer: 158.

Circular Tour   *2 points*
··

It has often been observed that individuals lost in a desert will set off with the intention of walking in a straight line but will eventually return to their starting point. Why is this?

Clue: 106/Answer: 150.

Radio Broadcast

2 *points*

One summer a Polish radio station, in an attempt to render a service to listeners, broadcasted a noise which was proven to deter mosquitoes while not bothering humans. The station received a barrage of complaints from listeners. Why?

Clue: 127/Answer: 167.

A Riddle

2 *points*

An old riddle goes like this:

A man without eyes, saw plums on a tree.
He did not take plums and he did not leave plums. How could this be?

Clue: 128/Answer: 168.

A Door Too Large   *2 points*

A man bought a door to fit in a door frame. The door was too large, so he cut off a piece. He found it was too small. So he cut off another piece. This time the door fitted perfectly. How come? (He cut pieces only off the door, he did not cut the frame.)

Clue: 108/Answer: 152.

Hide-and-Seek   *2 points*

The children had been playing hide-and-seek for some time when Jackie said, "I can't play anymore. It is obvious that anyone could find me now." "It depends who is doing the seeking," said Joan. "Most of us would find you easily, but for John it would be just as hard to find you as anyone else who was hiding." She was right. What was going on?

Clue: 114/Answer: 157.

Dance Ban   *2 points*

A bar in Rio has a regular dance competition every Thursday night. It banned one man from entering because he kept winning. He was not a professional dancer or schooled in dancing. Why did he keep winning?

Clue: 107/Answer: 151.

The Missing Money

2 points

A man went to a cash-dispensing machine outside a New York bank and withdrew $200, which he carefully put into the back pocket of his trousers. He spent $30 that day. The next day, when he reached into the back pocket of his trousers, he found only $5. Nobody had robbed him. What had happened?

Clue: 119/Answer: 161.

500 Times

2 points

Florence has 500 times as many as Washington. Of what?

Clue: 111/Answer: 155.

Bouncing Baby

2 points

How could a baby fall out of a twenty-story building and live?

Clue: 102/Answer: 147.

The Tower

2 points

A man went to the top of a 180-foot-high cylindrical tower. He leapt off, but was uninjured. Why?

Clue: 135/Answer: 175.

The Drive   *2 points*

A man and woman in a car drove down the drive from their house to the road. The man was behind the wheel. When they reached the road they got out and changed places. The woman turned the car around, then they swapped places again and the man drove back down the drive to the house. They did this several times. Why?

Clue: 109/Answer: 152.

The Slow-Car Race   *2 points*

A special endurance test involved two drivers and their

cars. They were told to drive one hundred miles out into the desert, rest for no more than one hour, and then drive back. The catch was that the last car back would be the winner.

The two drove out very slowly. During the rest period, one of the drivers began to doze. The other driver immediately drove back as fast as he could. Why did he do this?

Clue: 131/Answer: 171.

Homecoming   2 *points*
···

An executive who was based in New York was posted to Hong Kong on an assignment. When he was due to return, he faxed his manager the following request: "Is it OK for me to transport back to New York, at the company's expense, my personal items, household effects, and junk?" He was given approval and did so.

A furious argument ensued. The company refused to pay the transportation charge and, in the end, the executive had to sue the company. He won, but that is not the issue. The question is: What was the cause of the argument?

Clue: 115/Answer: 158.

Bypass   2 *points*
···

The people of a small French town were very annoyed by the traffic, especially the heavy trucks, that travelled the one main road running through the town. To eliminate the problem, they built a modern bypass road that was much wider than the road through the town. However, they soon found that they got at least as many trucks going through the town as before. Why?

Clue: 104/Answer: 149.

People Puzzles

The Postman   *2 points*

A postman had to deliver a letter to a house that was surrounded by a five-foot wall. The house could be
approached only by the main path. Unfortunately, a fero-
cious dog was tied by a long lead to a tree nearby, so that
the path was well within the dog's range. If the postman
walked up the path, he was sure to be attacked by the dog.
How did he outmaneuver the dog and deliver the letter?

Clue: 126/Answer: 166.

The Boss   *2 points*

One day a boss said to his employees, "I can fight and beat
any man who works here." A new employee, a seven-foot-
tall ex-prizefighter, stood up to take on the boss. What did
the boss do?

Clue: 102/Answer: 147.

The Stockbroker   *2 points*

Why did a stockbroker continue to send out to many people forecasts of stock price movements that he knew
would be wrong?

Clue: 133/Answer: 172.

The Runner   *2 points*

When a runner reached the end of a long, gruelling marathon, officials were amazed to see him continue to run. Why did he do this?

Clue: 128/Answer: 169.

The Ventriloquist   *2 points*

It was only when he died that the secret of a great ventriloquist was discovered. What was it?

Clue: 138/Answer: 177.

The Golfer
3 points

Jones was playing in a golf match that he very much wanted to win. He was on the green and using his putter. He carefully lined up his putt, aimed at the hole, and then deliberately putted the ball right over and beyond the hole. Why did he do this?

Clue: 113/Answer: 156.

The Professors
3 points

Two professors of mathematics glared at each other as they examined the same elementary equation. It had been written by a ten-year-old child. "This equation is correct," said one. "No, it is absolutely wrong," said the other. How could two experts disagree so completely about a simple equation?

Clue: 126/Answer: 167.

The Quatorzième
3 points

In Paris, a man with a job known as a *quatorzième* sits in his place of work in the evening. Sometimes he is called on to do something, but most evenings he is not. What does he do?

Clue: 127/Answer: 167.

The Cartoonist
3 points

Why does the United States Air Force employ the services of a top-class cartoonist?

Clue: 105/Answer: 149.

The Swimmer

3 points

In 1967, Sylvia Ester, an East German Olympic swimmer, swam the one hundred-meter freestyle in a time of 57.9 seconds, a new world record. But this was never recognized or acknowledged. Why not?

Clue: 134/Answer: 174.

The Climber

3 points

A climber bought an expensive new pair of climbing boots. On his first outing with them he found that they were too tight, so he changed into some old boots he had brought. He did not want to carry the new boots all the way up the mountain and back, but he feared that if he left them behind they would be found and kept by another climber. What did he do?

Clue: 106/Answer: 150.

The Salesman

3 points

A door-to-door salesman visited a house in order to demonstrate an excellent new model of vacuum cleaner. As part of the demonstration, he emptied a small bag of soot on a carpet. To his embarrassment the vacuum cleaner would not pick up the soot. Why not?

Clue: 129/Answer: 169.

The Secretary

3 points

A secretary went on vacation. She inadvertently took with

her something from the office. Her boss sent her a message asking her to return it immediately. This she did. Yet, when she returned from vacation, she was dismissed. Why?

Clue: 129/Answer: 169.

The Millionaire   4 points

A man working late at the office left some sandwiches on his desk. As a result of this, he later became a multimillionaire. How?

Clue: 119/Answer: 161.

The Engineer   *4 points*

An engineer was studying a dam when he was suddenly killed. How?

Clue: 109/Answer: 153.

The Farmer   *4 points*

A greedy and miserly farmer worked hard and tended his crops very carefully. Suddenly, he dashed out one day and dug up a field that had a crop of half-grown hay. It was a little wet, but there was nothing wrong with the crop. He subsequently had to resow the field, and the whole episode cost him much time and money. Why did he do it?

Clue: 110/Answer: 154.

The Investigator   *4 points*

A private investigator followed a man. He waited until the man parked his car and went off. The investigator then let the air out of one of the tires on the man's car. Waiting at a distance, he watched as the man returned, examined the flat tire, and then walked off. The investigator then went home, pleased with his day's work. What had he been hired to do?

Clue: 116/Answer: 159.

WALLY Test III

Now is the time to test your wits with a quick-fire WALLY test. Get out a pencil and paper and write down the answers to the following questions. You have two minutes to complete the test. Answers cannot be changed once written down and you must not look at any of the solutions until you have completed the test. Be warned that WALLY tests sometimes contain trick questions of a kind designed to catch you out!

1. On which side of a cup is it best to have the handle?
2. Where do the biggest potatoes grow?
3. Who was the first man mentioned in the Bible?
4. Where did Noah strike the last nail in the ark?
5. What living thing has only one foot?
6. What did Paul Revere say at the end of his epic ride?
7. Would you rather a tiger attack you or a lion?
8. What is it that Adam, the first man, never had and never saw yet he left to his children?
9. What kind of dog, found in every country, has legs but never runs?
10. Where are all men equally good-looking?

See WALLY Test solutions on page 181.

Crime Puzzles

Robbery *2 points*

A gang of criminals was loading a van with television sets that they were stealing from a warehouse when they suddenly heard the siren of an approaching police car. They could not avoid or outpace the police car. How did they escape?

Clue: 128/Answer: 168.

Great Detection   *2 points*

. . . .

A masked robber passed a note to a bank teller. It said, "I've got a gun. Hand over all the money in your till." The teller did so and the robber made good his escape. Within twenty-four hours, the police had arrested him. What mistake had he made?

Clue: 114/Answer: 157.

Headline News   *2 points*

. . . .

A jury found John Jones guilty of murder, and the judge passed the death penalty on him. The judge then returned to his chambers, sat down for a cup of coffee, and picked up a copy of the afternoon paper. The headline read, "John Jones Guilty—Sentenced to Death." The judge was baffled that the paper could have printed the story in so short a time. How could they?

Clue: 114/Answer: 157.

The Bad Driver   *2 points*

. . . .

James was a notoriously bad driver. He always drove much faster than the speed limit, through red traffic lights, and up one-way streets the wrong way. He was known to the police as the worst and most dangerous driver in town. Yet, for twenty years, he did not have any kind of motoring accident, was not arrested or cautioned by the police, and kept a clean license. How come?

Clue: 101/Answer: 146.

Point-Blank Shot   *3 points*

A man walked up to a naked woman, pointed a gun at her heart, and shot her. She survived. How?

Clue: 124/Answer: 165.

The Trial   *3 points*

A man was on trial for the murder of another man, despite the fact that the body had not been found. During the trial there was a sensational announcement that the man who had been murdered was, in fact, alive and in the next five seconds was about to enter the courtroom. The murdered man, however, did not arrive, and the prosecutor then claimed he could prove the defendant guilty. How?

Clue: 136/Answer: 175.

The Forger   *2 points*

A forger spent years studying the U.S. $100 bill until he produced what he felt was a perfect forgery. However, he was arrested the first time he tried to pass one. Why?

Clue: 111/Answer: 155.

Poisoned   *3 points*

An old man was poisoned. The police found that he had eaten and drunk nothing on the day of his death. How had the poison been administered?

Clue: 125/Answer: 165.

The Unhappy Patient   *3 points*

A man suffering from pains was examined by a doctor who correctly diagnosed the condition. The doctor did nothing. The pain went away. The man was unhappy. Why?

Clue: 137/Answer: 176.

The Unsuccessful Robbery   *3 points*

A gang of armed robbers burst into a large bank. They demanded all the money from the tills. The bank manager pointed out that there was none. They then insisted that he open the safe. He did so but there was no money inside. Just then the police arrived and arrested the gang. What was going on?

Clue: 138/Answer: 177.

The Burglary   *4 points*

A couple went on holiday, leaving their house empty but well secured. They had left their keys with a very careful and honest neighbor. When they returned, they found that they had been robbed of many valuables including jewelry, video equipment, etc. There was no sign of any break-in. How had it happened?

Clue: 103/Answer: 147.

Murder

An elderly woman is found dead in her bed. She has been murdered. In her bedroom is a fine collection of plates. The police established that she was in good health, seemed perfectly fine when she went shopping the day before, and that no one else had recently visited or entered the house. How did she die?

Clue: 120/Answer: 162.

The Golden Vase

4 points

A very valuable golden vase was in the middle of a large

room in a museum. It was surrounded by an electronic field that formed a complete sphere around the vase. If anything pierced the electronic field, the alarm bells would ring and guards appear in seconds. An enterprising thief worked out a way to break into the museum, but he knew that, if he set off the alarm, the guards would arrive before he could escape with the vase. How did he steal the vase and escape without being caught?

Clue: 113/Answer: 156.

A Shooting   *4 points*

At a party two men, Rob and Bill, became engaged in a violent quarrel. Rob pulled a gun and, in plain view of many witnesses, shot Bill dead. The police were called. They questioned Rob and the witnesses. They decided that it was a case of murder, yet they pressed no charge against Rob. Why not?

Clue: 130/Answer: 170.

Another Shooting   *4 points*

A police officer shot a woman dead. Someone else was charged with her murder and found guilty. How come?

Clue: 100/Answer: 145.

Speeding   *4 points*

A man who was driving well in excess of the speed limit was chased by a police car for several miles. Then the man saw another police car in front of him on the road so he pulled over. The officers from both cars came over to him. They had both clearly seen him speeding, yet neither arrested him nor gave him a ticket. They simply gave him a warning and let him go. Why?

Clue: 132/Answer: 172.

Difficult Puzzles

Export Drive   3 *points*
....

During the 1930s, how did some Japanese businessmen overcome American mistrust of goods made in Japan?

Clue: 110/Answer: 153.

Bombs Away   3 *points*
....

A bomber plane, which was in perfect working order, was over its target. The tea that the pilot had been drinking sat in its cup at his elbow. The plane released its bombs, but they did not fall from the plane. Why not?

Clue: 102/Answer: 146.

Space Shuttle   3 *points*
....

Why is it that a plane is allowed to take off and fly in a thunderstorm, but the space shuttle is not?

Clue: 132/Answer: 171.

Small Furniture

3 points

A factory specializes in producing furniture that is twenty percent smaller than normal furniture. The furniture is not designed for or sold especially to smaller-sized people. Why do they make it?

Clue: 132/Answer: 171.

Suspense

3 points

A man traveling by train awoke to find his railcar suspended twenty feet in the air. Why?

Clue: 134/Answer: 174.

The Woman in the Ditch
3 *points*
• •

A beautiful woman walked across a field several times. She deliberately walked in a six-inch ditch. Why?

Clue: 140/Answer: 178.

Grease
3 *points*
• •

A man covered the head of a stranger in grease. Why?

Clue: 113/Answer: 157.

Cash in Hand
3 *points*
• •

Smith had owed Jones a thousand dollars and, although Jones asked for the sum many times, Smith never paid it back. Then one day Smith offered to repay Jones the thousand dollars in cash, but Jones refused to accept it. Why?

Clue: 105/Answer: 150.

The Nosy Student
3 *points*
• •

Judy, a young woman studying at college, was unfortunate to have a roommate who was rude, lazy, selfish, and inquisitive. Judy was annoyed because, while she was at lectures, her roommate would look through Judy's desk and read Judy's personal mail. How did Judy overcome this problem?

Clue: 122/Answer: 163.

Anywhere in the World   *3 points*

. . . .

A pilot was due to fly his plane from one place to another when a man asked if he could be given a lift. The pilot said, "Yes, for a small fee that is possible. I can drop you off on my way." "But you don't know where I am going," replied the man. "Surely that makes a big difference." "Not at all," said the pilot. How could this be so?

Clue: 100/Answer: 145.

Poor Equipment   *3 points*

. . . .

A man took an expensive piece of equipment with him on

a journey. When he reached his destination he found that the equipment, though in perfect working order, was of practically no use. Why not?

Clue: 125/Answer: 166.

Stand at the Back   3 *points*
••

During a flight from Brazil to London, the pilot told all the passengers to get out of their seats and to stand at the back of the plane. Why did he do this?

Clue: 132/Answer: 172.

Police Visit   3 *points*
••

Before you can buy a car in Tokyo, the police must first come and visit you. Why?

Clue: 125/Answer: 165.

Large and Small   3 *points*
••

Why, on the same day, were several groups of strong, fit, large people taking instructions from puny, small people?

Clue: 117/Answer: 159.

The Book   3 *points*
••

A man walked into a bookshop and bought a book even

though he could not understand a word of the language in which the entire book was written. Why did he buy it?

Clue: 102/Answer: 147.

Pentagon Panic

3 points

One day during the cold war, a young officer rushed into his superior's office in the United States Department of Defense in Washington, D.C. "We have discovered," he said, "that if both we and the Russians launch our missiles at exactly the same time, their missiles would hit the United States before our missiles hit Russia." "Are our missiles slower?" asked his superior. "No, they have exactly the same power, weight, and speed." "Is the distance they fly shorter?" "No, both distances flown are exactly the same." "Well, what is the reason?" Can you tell?

Clue: 124/Answer: 165.

Page 78 *3 points*

Every week a woman went into the local library. If she saw a book that looked interesting, she immediately turned to page 78 before deciding whether she should borrow the book or not. Why?

Clue: 123/Answer: 164.

The Statue **3 points**

A huge and very heavy statue had to be lifted onto a large pedestal base in the middle of a town square. The bottom of the statue was completely flat and there was no way of lifting it except by putting ropes around and under it. How did they manage to get the ropes out from under the statue once it was lifted onto the base?

Clue: 133/Answer: 172.

The Service *3 points*

A man regularly used and paid for a particular service that was provided by a large organization. The organization announced that, as a special promotion, it would offer all customers the service for one week at one-tenth of the normal price. The man refused this offer and continued to pay the normal price during the special promotion week. Why did he do this?

Clue: 129/Answer: 169.

Historical Puzzles

Jam Doughnut   *2 points*
....

Why did a famous statesman and world leader stand up in front of a large group of people and say, very seriously, "I am a jam doughnut"?

Clue: 116/Answer: 159.

Without Drought   *2 points*
....

How did the American Civil War lead to a reduction in droughts in various parts of the world?

Clue: 140/Answer: 178.

Cross the Gorge   *3 points*
....

It was decided to build a suspension bridge over a deep and wide gorge. The river at the bottom of the gorge was too violent for any boat to cross. How did the engineers get the heavy cables from one side of the gorge to the other?

Clue: 106/Answer: 151.

The End of the War   *2 points*

How do we know that the war between Lydia and Media in Asia Minor ended on precisely May 28, 585 B.C., in our dating system?

Clue: 109/Answer: 153.

The Stiff Gate   *3 points*

Several people were invited to dinner in a private house. They found that it was quite difficult to open the front gate as it was very stiff. At dinner, one of the guests commented on this and the host smiled. He then explained why he had made the gate hard to open. What was the explanation?

Clue: 133/Answer: 172.

The Twelve   *3 points*

From the beginning of time and up to the time of this writing, twelve and only twelve people have achieved this feat. What is it?

Clue: 136/Answer: 175.

Across the River   *3 points*

In the early days of exploration in America, a group of explorers came to a deep, wide river. There was no bridge, and they had no boats or material to make boats. They could not swim. How did they get across?

Clue: 98/Answer: 144.

Brunelleschi's Challenge   3 *points*

Filippo Brunelleschi is one of the great figures of the Italian Renaissance; he was a sculptor, goldsmith, and architect. His greatest masterpiece is the dome of the cathedral in Florence, which he completed in 1417. He had to win the commission for the dome against stiff competition. The story is told that he won by issuing a challenge to his competitors to stand an egg upright on a flat table without using any other materials. No one else could do it. How did Brunelleschi do it?

Clue: 103/Answer: 147.

Houdini's Challenge   3 *points*

The great conjurer and escapologist Harry Houdini was an expert with locks and safes. He was once challenged by a safe manufacturer to open a locked safe. Before accepting the challenge, Houdini examined the safe carefully and saw that it was of a new design that he would almost certainly find impossible to unlock. Nevertheless, he accepted the challenge, and won it. How?

Clue: 115/Answer: 158.

The Building   3 *points*

A man was very relieved one day to reach a building and go inside. It was a place he normally disliked. There was no one there to meet him, and there was nothing for him to do there. Why was he so pleased?

Clue: 103/Answer: 147.

The Forgery   *4 points*

A historical researcher was presented with a document purported to be an authentic mid-eighteenth-century bill signed by the King of England. How did he know at once that it was a forgery?

Clue: 111/Answer: 155.

The Impostor   *4 points*

A woman once came forward and claimed to be Anastasia, heiress to the Russian throne. How did the authorities quickly discover that she was an impostor?

Clue: 116/Answer: 159.

Motionless   *4 points*

A young man combed his hair and then sat in a chair for twenty minutes without moving a muscle. Why did he do this?

Clue: 120/Answer: 162.

The Courtier   *4 points*

King Alfonso XIII of Spain (1886–1931) apparently employed a man at court with just one specific function in relation to music. What was that function?

Clue: 106/Answer: 151.

Homing Spaniards

4 points

During the early days of their conquests of Central and South America, Spanish soldiers often had to travel long distances through strange, uncharted country. Sometimes they travelled at night. They developed an excellent method of ensuring that they could always find their way back to their base. How?

Clue: 115/Answer: 158.

WALLY Test IV

Now for another WALLY test. Get a pencil and paper and give your best answers to the following questions. You have two minutes!

1. How can you drop a raw egg onto a concrete floor without cracking it?
2. If it took eight men ten hours to build a wall, how long would it take four men to build it?
3. Which would you prefer to have, an old ten-dollar bill or a new one?
4. Approximately how many birthdays does the average Japanese woman have?
5. If you had three apples and four oranges in one hand and four apples and three oranges in the other hand, what would you have?
6. How can you lift an elephant with one hand?
7. What do you always get hanging from apple trees?
8. How can a man go eight days without sleep?
9. Why are so many famous artists Dutch?
10. Divide twenty by a half and add ten. What is the answer?

See WALLY Test solutions on page 182.

Gruesome Puzzles

Ageless
2 points

A young couple were separated shortly after they met and they did not come face to face again for fifty years. By that time he had become an old man, but she had not aged at all. In fact, she looked exactly as he had seen her fifty years before. Why?

Clue: 98/Answer: 144.

The Rock
2 points

A man, going about his business, brushed against a rock. Within minutes he was dead. Why?

Clue: 128/Answer: 169.

The Breeze
2 points

A man was standing up on a bright sunny day, happy to feel the breeze in his face. He knew that if the wind dropped he would die. Why?

Clue: 103/Answer: 147.

The Accident
2 points

A careless driver caused an accident. Fortunately, both he and the driver of the other car were wearing seat belts and

were uninjured. However, a passenger in the other car (who was not wearing a seat belt) was very badly mangled in the accident and lost both his legs as a result. When the case came to court the careless driver escaped with a small fine. Why was the judge so lenient?

Clue: 98/Answer: 144.

The Nonchalant Wife

3 points

A woman came home one evening and switched on the light in her living room. She was horrified to see the remains of her husband lying on the floor. He had committed suicide. Ignoring the situation, the woman had a cup of coffee and went calmly about her housework, and did not phone for medical assistance or the police. Why not?

Clue: 121/Answer: 163.

Two Men   *3 points*

A man died a nasty death and another man many miles away was at last happy even though they had never met and no grudges were borne. What was going on?

Clue: 136/Answer: 175.

Too Polite   *3 points*

Japanese office workers strive to be very polite. One was killed because he was too polite. How?

Clue: 135/Answer: 175.

The Deadly Climb   *4 points*

A group of healthy men walked up a mountain. One of them died. If the man who died had climbed the mountain on any other day, he would have lived. What happened?

Clue: 108/Answer: 152.

The Cruel King   *3 points*

Two men were asked by their king to carry out a certain

task. They did this entirely to his satisfaction and went to him seeking their just reward. However, the king decreed instead that they both be severely punished. Why did he do this?

Clue: 107/Answer: 151.

Dead Man, Dead Dog   *4 points*

A man and his dog were found dead in the middle of a field. The man was wearing wading boots. No one else was around. How had they died?

Clue: 108/Answer: 152.

Axe Attack   *4 points*

A woman knocked on a stranger's door and asked to use the bathroom. She came out and killed the man with an axe. Why?

Clue: 100/Answer: 145.

A Mysterious Death   *4 points*

A healthy man went out for a walk one evening and was later found dead. The police examined the body carefully but were mystified as to the cause of death. No one else was involved. A postmortem revealed that the man had been killed by a freak accident that left virtually no trace. What was it?

Clue: 120/Answer: 162.

The Man Who Shot Himself   *4 points*

A man who was alone in a room very carefully and deliberately pulled out a gun and shot himself. Some time later, another man was charged with his murder and found guilty. What happened?

Clue: 118/Answer: 161.

Fiendish Puzzles

Light Saving   *4 points*

In the subway of a major American city, the stealing of light bulbs was a common occurrence and a major problem. The sockets for the light bulbs were within easy reach and could not be moved. How did the city authorities solve this problem and practically eliminate the theft of light bulbs?

Clue: 117/Answer: 160.

Matchless   *4 points*

A particular person born in January 1978 has a unique distinction. What is it?

Clue: 118/Answer: 161.

The Less-Costly Capital   *4 points*

One of the world's capital cities spends much less (both as a proportion of its budget and in absolute terms) than other capital cities on a social service which is generally considered vital. Why is this?

Clue: 117/Answer: 160.

An Odd Number
4 points

What is peculiar about the number 8549176320?

Clue: 122/Answer: 164.

Bus Stop I
4 points

A man is standing at a bus stop carrying an ordinary kitchen chair in his hands. Why?

Clue: 104/Answer: 148.

Stop/Go
4 points

A group of responsible people, not pranksters, drive around a city in their car. When they stop for a traffic light, they do not go, even if the light has turned green, until a car behind them toots its horn. Why do they do this?

Clue: 133/Answer: 173.

Vanishing Point
4 points

A man paid a great deal of money to travel to an exotic location, but when he returned he found that he had never really been there at all. Why? Where was it?

Clue: 138/Answer: 176.

Bus Stop II
4 points

A woman travels by bus to a certain building every day.

There are two bus stops on her side of the street. One is one hundred yards before the building and the other is 200 yards beyond the building. She always gets off at the bus stop two hundred yards past the building and walks back. Why?

Clue: 104/Answer: 148.

One Inch Shorter   4 points

A man went to work one day and by the end of his day's work he was one inch shorter. Why?

Clue: 123/Answer: 164.

The Signal   *4 points*

John stood in an enclosed room watched by three men.
The room had no windows or openings, but solid walls,
floor, ceiling, and door. There was no telephone or electrical device of any kind. The three men (who all had good
eyesight and hearing) watched John carefully in silence.
They observed no change in condition, sound, or move-
ment. Yet, while they were watching, John signalled to his
partner, James, in a nearby room and passed a message to
him. How?

Clue: 131/Answer: 171.

Western Sunrise   *4 points*

As we all know, the sun rises every day in the east and
sets in the west. One day, a man saw the sun rise in the
west. How?

Clue: 139/Answer: 178.

Teenage Party   *4 points*

While his parents were away, a teenage boy and his
friends drank some of the parents' gin. This was of course
strictly forbidden. They then poured water into the gin
bottle to return the level to where it had originally been,
and put the bottle back exactly where they had found it.
However, when the couple came home, the father took
one look at the bottle of gin and turned angrily to his son
to denounce him for illicit drinking. How had he known?

Clue: 135/Answer: 174.

THE CLUES

The Accident

The driver's car was white. The other car was black.

Acidic Action

He disposed of her clothes and jewelry.

Her body was completely dissolved in acid.

A trace of her was found and identified.

Across the River

They got across without getting wet.

They did not use any additional materials, but crossed the deep, wide river easily.

Adolf Hitler

It was the real Adolf Hitler, the one who led the German Third Reich.

Adolf Hitler was alive at the time, and the war still had much time to run.

The British soldier did not recognize Hitler. But it would have made no difference if he had.

Adrift in the Ocean

They found a source of drinking water.

No rain or ice is involved.

They were in a particular location.

Ageless

They had been involved in an accident. He had aged, but she was perfectly preserved.

Alex Ferguson

Soccer is played in Singapore.

Alex Ferguson's style of coaching would be appropriate.

One of his personal habits would not be acceptable in Singapore.

Alone in a Boat

They were deliberately cast adrift from a famous boat.

The animals can sometimes offend the senses.

Ancient Antics

It has to do with nourishment.

It does not involve a particular strength or physical skill.

It concerns animals.

Angry Response

She was angry because he was late.

They had no particular appointment at eight o'clock.

Another Shooting

The policeman did not shoot the woman deliberately.

The man who was found guilty of the woman's murder had placed her in danger.

The police were trying to save the woman.

Anywhere in the World

The pilot was due to fly from one place to another so that, wherever the passenger wanted to go, it would be on the pilot's route, and dropping the passenger off would hardly make any difference to the pilot's total flight time.

Think of the Earth as a sphere.

Assault and Battery

John is healthy.

The person who hits John does it to help him.

It is a common occurrence.

The Auction

He was bidding for a pet.

The creature had a talent.

He thought he was in a competitive auction.

Axe Attack

When the woman entered the house she had no idea who the man was and had no intention of doing him any harm.

It was while the woman was in the bathroom that she realized who the man was and decided to kill him.

The woman had seen the axe before.

The Bad Driver

Although he always drove badly, he committed no offense in this twenty-year period.

Bald Facts

Her hair loss was part of a greater misfortune that befell her.

She did not lose her hair from natural causes.

Her choice of lover was important.

Bare Bones

The student was healthy and was not physically abnormal.

She had never had any kind of medical operation.

Every human is born with two femurs.

Barren Patch

The patch of land received the same sunlight and rain as the fertile land around it.

The patch is an irregular shape.

No one had ever gone there, but human action had made the land barren.

Biography

His death was accidental.

Had he chosen a different subject for a biography, he would not have died.

The author died a similar death to that suffered by the subject of his biography.

Bombs Away

The bomber was in the air at a height of 20,000 feet and over its target. It was flying right-way-up (unlike a similar, classic puzzle where the pilot could not be having tea). The mechanism was in working order, but the bombs, when released, did not fall from the plane.

The bombs fell.

The Book

He did not buy it for the pictures, illustrations, style, or appearance of the book. Nor did he have any intention of reading it or learning the language it was written in.

He was thrilled to get the book and eager to show it to his friends.

The Boss

The boss kept his word, but did not beat the man or back down.

Bottled Up

The bottles remained unbroken, unchanged, and unused throughout.

They were worthless when empty, but had been expensive when full.

She was status-conscious.

Bouncing Baby

The baby was a normal human baby and it fell onto the hard sidewalk, but lived.

The Breeze

He was standing still but moving slowly.

Brunelleschi's Challenge

The table was flat and horizontal. The egg was a regular hen's egg, not cooked or treated in any way. He made the egg stand on the table without any other materials or items.

The other contestants made an assumption about what they were allowed to do. This assumption stopped them from seeing the solution that Brunelleschi used.

The Building

He was a thief who had fled.

This took place many years ago.

The Burglary

The neighbor had allowed access in, but had watched every action they made like a hawk.

Something had apparently been delivered in error.

Valuable pictures, which were mounted high on the wall, had not been stolen.

Burnt Wood

The wood has a symbolic value, but is not in itself rare or valuable.

The men involved in this quest all speak English yet come from countries far apart.

They compete over many weeks.

Bus Stop I

The man would have liked to have sat on the chair while he waited for the bus, but he could not.

The man was unhappy, and the chair was the cause of his unhappiness.

When he got on the bus, the man had difficulty paying his fare.

Bus Stop II

The woman does not meet anybody or pass anything of interest or benefit to her by going to the farther bus stop. She does not like exercise.

When the woman comes home, she walks to the nearer bus stop in order to catch the bus.

The woman finds it easier to walk two hundred yards from the far bus stop, rather than one hundred yards from the near bus stop.

Business Rivalry

Cain uses Abel's lower prices to his own personal advantage.

Cain changes his profession.

They were competitors in the early days of the railroad business.

Bypass

In this true incident, trucks continued to pour through the town, although cars used the new road.

The Carpet Seller

The solution can be accomplished in a single cut, but it is not a straight cut.

The two pieces can fit together perfectly to make either a nineby sixteen rectangle or a twelve by twelve square.

The carpet is not used on the stairs, but it may be helpful to think in terms of steps!

The Cartoonist

The cartoonist is employed to draw cartoons, but not for entertainment or amusement.

The cartoons are used in pilot training.

Cartoon Character

The scientific journal misstated and exaggerated the properties of something.

The cartoon character was designed to be a sort of role model for children, and to influence their habits.

The cartoon character was intended to make an unpopular but healthy item popular.

Cash in Hand

Smith offered to pay Jones the thousand dollars at a time when it would have been disadvantageous for Jones to accept it.

Whichever of them had the money would lose it shortly.

Chimney Problem

He came down very slowly.

The chimney was not the same after he finished his descent.

Circular Tour

What we think of as equal are often not equal.

Clean Shaven

Alexander the Great was interested in military conquest.

He believed that clean-shaven soldiers had an advantage.

The Climber

He hid the boots, but in a way that, even if they were found, it was unlikely they would be taken.

They were a fine pair of climbing boots.

Complete Garbage

If the garbage had not been emptied, he would have lived.

He was poor and tired.

He died a violent death.

The Courtier

The courtier did not have any particular musical skill, but he had a good memory.

The king had a particular affliction.

The courtier was called into use on certain state occasions.

Cross the Gorge

This happened over a hundred years ago, before planes or rockets could be used. The engineers could cross the gorge only by travelling miles downstream.

Just as the world's entire population is descended from Adam and Eve, so a small beginning can lead to a great outcome.

The Cruel King

The king did not punish the men for any wrongdoing on their part, but rather for his own selfish reasons.

Their punishment was execution. It meant that they could never present a threat to the king.

The king was miserly, selfish, cruel, and very rich.

Dali's Brother

Salvador Dali is recognized as a brilliant surrealist painter.

Salvador Dali's younger brother was actually a brilliant surrealist painter but his older brother never knew this.

The two brothers had something important and unusual in common.

Dance Ban

The other contestants thought he used a low trick, but it was really just a natural advantage in this kind of dance.

A Day at the Races

The man deserved to be punished.

He had no special influence with the police, and they fully intended to prosecute him.

He had a special skill that he often used to his advantage.

The Deadly Climb

Climbing conditions were perfect as the men all walked up the high mountain. The dead man's companions were unharmed, but he died a painful death.

The man was an enthusiastic, all-round sportsman. He climbed the mountain in the afternoon.

It was what the man did in the morning which lead to his death on the mountain.

Dead Man, Dead Dog

The man had been fishing illegally in a lake.

In desperation the man had run away from the lake, but to no avail.

The dog was a retriever.

Debugging

Ants were used in the diagnosis of diabetes.

The ants' actions could indicate that a person had diabetes.

Don't Get Up

No one else is in the apartment and she knows that no one else will answer the phone.

She does not know the caller, but she knows that the call is probably important.

She knows the call is not for her.

She has no malicious motives.

A Door Too Large

He had to take two cuts from the door to make it fit. Both

cuts were from the length of the door. The width and thickness remained the same.

The Drive

They had never done this before, but once they started they followed this same procedure for several weeks: swapping places where the drive met the road. Then they never did it again.

88 Too Big

It was a number he chose to use.

He was not at home.

He did not know the right number.

The End of the War

An unusual event marked the end of the war. It is an event that nowadays we can date with great precision.

The Engineer

He stood on the river bank watching the dam, which was in excellent condition.

He was killed accidentally by one of the dam's constructors.

Although he had heard about this kind of dam before, he had never seen one and he marvelled at its construction. No mechanical aids or formal training had been used.

Exceptional Gratitude

Bill thanked Ted for eggs he had never received in order to influence Ted's actions.

They were neighbors.

Ted was lazy and mean.

Export Drive

They relocated their premises within Japan.

They made a true but misleading statement on their goods.

Fair Fight

The boxer did not expect to collect any money.

The trainer collected a worthwhile sum for his efforts.

The boxer won fairly, but without throwing a punch.

The Farmer

He had had no intention of ploughing up the field until he had awoken that morning.

He ruined the crops in the forlorn hope of a much larger harvest.

He was superstitious.

Fill Her Up!

He deliberately ruined the car, but later he deeply regretted his action.

He was a jealous cement truck driver.

Fingerprint Evidence

It was not Bundy's fingerprints or any of his victim's fingerprints that incriminated him, but it was fingerprint evidence.

The police found something unusual when they searched Bundy's apartment.

Fired for Joining Mensa

Anne's employers would not have objected to her joining any other organization.

She was employed in an administrative position, she did her job well, and her employers were pleased with her.

If she had joined Mensa, there may have been a conflict of interest.

500 Times

This is a physical difference and, for the purposes of the puzzle, it may be assumed that Florence and Washington are about the same size and age.

Flipping Pages

I did this deliberately in order to produce a specific result.

I could do this only in certain places.

I should have gotten permission from the publisher first.

The Forger

He was nearly arrested for a driving offense that very morning.

The Forgery

There was nothing wrong with the general appearance of the document, the paper it was on, or the signature of the king.

The date on the document indicated to the expert that it was a forgery.

The date was a day in 1752, which would appear normal to many people. The expert knew that the document could not have been printed or signed on that particular date.

Free Lunch

The man ate his lunch with one knife and one fork.

He provided a service.

The restaurant provided an intimate atmosphere in the evenings.

Full Refund

It was highly unusual for the theater to give a refund.

The theater manager was glad that they left.

They had acted cruelly.

Garbage Nosiness

I was annoyed with myself, not with my neighbors.

I looked in the cans on the same morning each week.

When I looked in the cans, I saw that they had something in common, which mine did not.

Gas Attack

He did not use the mask to disguise himself or anyone else.

The gas mask was standard issue.

His actions could have saved the lives of many people.

Getting Away with Murder

The man had a long-standing motive to kill her.

He was clearly guilty, but had to be released under the law.

He was punished for this crime.

The Golden Vase

He hid in a small broom closet near the vase.

He came from Australia.

He convinced the guards that the alarm was faulty.

The Golfer

He was playing regular golf in which one plays from tee to green and tries to do so in the fewest strokes.

His previous shot had been a very poor one.

Golf Bag

Paul removed the bag without touching it.

He did not deliberately set fire to the bag since that would have incurred a penalty.

He indulged in a bad habit.

Grease

The man had a benevolent purpose in mind and the stranger was pleased to have the grease rubbed all over his head.

The man was in uniform, the stranger was not.

Great Detection

The police examined all clues left at the scene of the crime and quickly knew where they could find the robber.

The Great Wall

He had travelled a long way to see a sight that very few people have seen.

Happy Birthday

There was nothing about his appearance that indicated it was his birthday.

He was not well known.

She worked in a shop but was not a shop assistant.

She had access to information.

Headline News

The editor of the newspaper had not known what the jury's verdict would be, but he ensured that his newspaper was available, with the correct headline and story, as soon as the trial finished.

Hide-and-Seek

Jackie's condition had changed such that she was now much easier to find. John had a disability which gave him no advantage in finding Jackie.

High Blood Pressure

Gerald's blood pressure is normal for Gerald.

Hole in One

She hit one shot and her ball finished in the hole, but this did not count as a hole in one.

Homecoming

The cost of transporting the goods home was very high. The company claimed that the executive had misled them over what he wanted to bring back, but he showed the court that he had been accurate in his description.

Homing Spaniards

They did not mark the path in any particular way, nor did they memorize the route.

They rode out and rode back. No other people, birds, or animals served as guides.

Some of them rode stallions, but certainly not all of them did.

Hosing Down

They used regular water. The road was not contaminated in any way.

It was for a special event.

They did not hose the entire road.

Houdini's Challenge

He did not use any special equipment or explosive. He knew that he could not unlock the safe using a conventional approach, so he used a lateral approach.

Although the safe manufacturer and onlookers witnessed the feat, they could not see how Houdini managed to unlock the safe door.

The Impostor

The woman answered all their questions faultlessly and agreed to undergo any tests they requested.

The real Anastasia had a medical condition that would not have been immediately apparent even to a doctor. The woman underwent no medical tests.

Her agreement to take a test was seen as evidence that she was an impostor.

The Investigator

The private investigator had a camera.

The man was under investigation for fraud.

The investigator was gathering evidence for an insurance company.

Invisible

It can be made of metal or wood.

It is powerful.

You can see it under some circumstances, but not others, even when it is directly in front of you.

Jam Doughnut

He was in a foreign city.

Job Description

She acted on impulse, but she chose them for a specific reason.

The woman was angry because of the men's actions.

She knew they had been talking about her.

Large and Small

All the groups of people were engaged in the same activity.

The large, fit people were chosen for their strength. The small people were chosen for their light weight and their judgment.

Leadfoot and Gumshoe

She and the police officer were strangers and she was not trying to help or impress him.

She was acting from high moral principles, and was also protecting someone's reputation.

The Less-Costly Capital

The city spends less in this service area than other cities because it has less need to spend.

The service on which this capital city spends less is firefighting.

The city is not particularly cold or damp, yet its geography makes fires less likely.

Light Saving

The only thing that was changed was the design of the lightbulb and its socket.

The bulbs could still be removed by hand by the city engineers and maintenance staff.

The bulbs could be reached by hand by anyone, but the vandals found that, try as they might to unscrew the bulbs, they could not remove them.

Machine Forge

The man sells the machine to a crook.

Although the machine produces perfect $100 bills, it cannot be used to make the crook rich.

Man in Tights

He was knocked out by the rock, but it did not touch him.

He was involved in many dangerous adventures.

He was a well-known sight in his tights.

Man Overboard

The previous day he had bought some beautiful postcards of Jerusalem.

Matchless

The individual was the first person ever to have been born under certain circumstances.

From a medical or biological point of view, there was nothing unusual about the person's birth.

The location of the person's birth was singular.

The Man Who Got Water

He had intended to use the water in connection with his car, but something happened to make him change his mind.

He was very angry.

The Man Who Shot Himself

The man shot himself with his own gun and with the

immediate intention of killing himself. He had no history of suicidal tendencies, insanity, phobias, or psychological disorders.

The two men met shortly before the man shot himself. No words were spoken when they met, but because of the murderer's actions the man shot himself.

Both men were gangsters.

The Millionaire

The man is very famous.

The sandwiches that were left out were eaten by a visitor whose actions inspired the man.

He could draw very well.

Missing Items

He grows them.

Everyone has them—men and women.

They are in the lower part of the body.

The Missing Money

Nobody else was involved. At the end of the first day there was $170 in his trouser pocket. The next day he had $5 in his trouser pocket.

Misunderstood

Very few, if any, criminals speak this language.

It is chosen for its rarity.

A handful of words are used—but they are important.

Motionless

He was a perfectly healthy person and free to move, but he sat still voluntarily.

There was another person in the room. He was performing a service for the first man, but they never touched.

This took place during the nineteenth century.

Motion Not Passed

Many people voted for the motion, and the poll was performed correctly according to the rules.

If a few more people had voted against the motion, it would have been passed. If many more people had voted against it, then it would have been rejected.

Murder

The police discovered that she had been poisoned. They checked all the food and drink in the house and could find no trace of poison.

She had bought many fine plates, but rarely went to shops or markets.

The day before her death she had been to the grocery store and the post office.

A Mysterious Death

The man died an accidental but highly unusual death.

There was a tiny hole in his head.

Thousands fly through the air, but very few reach the ground.

No More Bore

Churchill gave the butler something.

The butler gave the impression that he was misbehaving.

The Nonchalant Wife

Even though she found her husband's remains on the floor, the woman had no reason to call any authorities.

The woman was horrified to see her husband's remains on the floor, but not at all surprised that he was dead.

Nonconventional

They are not prohibited from speaking altogether.

The do not use signs, gestures, or codes.

They are extremely courteous and concerned for the well-being of their companions.

Nonexistent Actors

The nonexistent actors had never existed and took no part whatsoever in the movie, but their names were put deliberately into the credits.

It was a murder-mystery movie.

No Response

The question was one that he often answered, and if anyone else had asked it he would have answered.

The content of the question does not matter. It was the way it was asked that matters.

The stranger had a difficulty.

The Nosy Student

Judy hid her letters in the shared room, but in a rather good hiding place.

The roommate was a very poor student.

Noteworthy

The criminal had committed a crime in the woman's house.

The criminal had visited the bank.

The picture of the president is well known.

November 11

Although it appeared as though many customers had been born on November 11, the real distribution of births of the company's customers was not unusual.

All the data had been entered on a computer database.

The customers appeared to have birthdays on November 11, 1911.

An Odd Number

You need no mathematical skills to solve this problem.

Note that each digit is used once.

The sequence of the digits is significant.

Once Too Often

You can do this many times in your life.

You do it on a specific day that is not of your choosing.

It is variously considered a right, a privilege, and a duty.

One Inch Shorter

The man was fit and healthy, as was necessary for his physically demanding job.

Nothing was cut off the man—he became an inch shorter as a result of an incident at work.

He was subjected to enormous forces.

One Mile

The one-mile kink is not associated with any physical or geographical feature of the landscape. The land there is the same as elsewhere along the border.

There was no mistake in the original map and none in the current map.

Actions were taken to speed up the survey of the border.

Page 78

She was not looking for a particular book, but for books in general that were interesting and new.

Her husband read the books.

Pass Protection

Other people could pass through in the same fashion that I did.

As I looked at the people in line, I could see the frustration in their faces.

I always buy a token for every journey.

Pentagon Panic

This has nothing to do with technology, rocket design, wind, or weather.

The same missile would get from Moscow to New York faster than it would get from New York to Moscow. If missiles were launched by both countries at the same time, the Russian missile would strike first. The reverse would be true for the same missiles going from Alaska to Vladivostock in eastern Russia. Then, the American missile would strike first.

Pentagon Puzzle

The number of people working there is not relevant.

The reason dates back to when the Pentagon was built.

When it was built, the extra bathrooms were necessary.

Picture Purchase

He was honest and there were no crooked motives involved.

He did not intend to take any action to make the picture more valuable.

He would not have bought the picture if it had been rolled up.

The Pilot's Son

No stepfathers, grandparents, or in-law relationships are involved. The passenger was the father of the pilot's son.

Point-Blank Shot

The gun was a real handgun in full working order, firing real bullets that would normally kill someone.

She was the kind of person who would make every effort to improve her career.

Poisoned

He had followed his normal daily routine unaware that someone had planned to poison him. He had met no one else on the day of his murder.

He had inadvertently put the poison into his mouth.

Police Visit

The purpose of the police visit has nothing to do with your driving skill or the condition of the car.

The population of Tokyo is over sixteen million people.

Poor Delivery

The misunderstanding was based on a problem with written communication. Each company followed exactly the same written instructions but interpreted them differently.

Poor Equipment

The piece of equipment was a watch.

The man took it somewhere on Earth where there is no official time.

Poor Investment

They could easily buy another of these items; in fact, they had several spare ones.

If it was lost, then it had to be found.

They were looking for information.

The Postman

He did not use anything to distract the dog except himself.

The Professors

The two professors each saw a simple written equation. But, for a very basic reason, they saw it differently. This made it right for one, but wrong for the other.

As they argued about this they looked straight at each other.

Promotion

The company knows exactly what John is like.

Promoting John is part of a clever plan.

They promote him very publicly.

The Power of Tourism

The tourists do not consume large amounts of electricity.

The place does not have costly lights or unusual electrical entertainment or appliances.

The place is a famous natural tourist attraction.

The Quatorzième

His work consists of eating a meal in a restaurant.

He always eats in a large group, but generally with people he has never met before and has nothing particularly in common with.

The Ransom Note

The police could glean no clues from the content, paper, or

style of the ransom note.

The ransom note was mailed, but the postmark gave no clues.

There were no fingerprints, but the police were able to establish a unique match with the criminal.

Radio Broadcast

The high-pitched noise achieved its intended purpose of driving off mosquitoes while being inaudible to humans.

Recovery

There was nothing wrong with the tow truck. The truck that had broken down had a serious fault which was remedied by the way they drove back.

Reentry

It is popular.

It is a collection.

Rejected Shoes

The shoes fit him comfortably, but there was something uncomfortable about them.

They were made of different material from his other shoes.

They were fine when worn outside, but not when worn inside.

Replacing the Leaves

The girl is very sad.

She is trying to prevent something from happening.

She is acting on something she heard.

A Riddle

He had sight and he took fruit.

Riddle of the Sphinx

The Sphinx had poetic license. Morning, afternoon, and evening are metaphorical rather than literal times.

Not all the legs are limbs, but they all support the body.

Right Off

He is upset that his new car is ruined, but pleased at something else.

No other vehicle is involved.

He acquires something rare.

Robbery

The gang did not attempt to flee. They thought laterally. The police did not.

The Rock

He was uninjured, but the rock damaged his suit.

The Runner

He knew that he had reached the end of the race, but he kept on running because he had a good reason to run.

Russian Racer

The papers reported accurately, but put the most positive light on the Russian car's performance and the most negative on the American car's.

The papers did not report how many cars raced.

The Salesman

There was nothing wrong with the vacuum cleaner. It was in perfect working order.

He had had a long drive to reach the house.

Scuba Do

He had not been diving and had no immediate intention of going diving.

He was an avid diver.

The reason had to do with safety.

The Secretary

She had taken a key. She posted it back immediately.

She was dismissed because she posted it back.

Secret Assignment

Knowing the students' habits, he did some clever detective work.

He knew they were serious, studious, and always prepared themselves for assignments.

He checked something in a particular place at the university.

The Service

The man paid more for the same service as everyone else in the expectation of future gain.

The man was a collector.

Seven Bells

The shopkeeper could easily change the sign, but chooses not to do so.

No superstition about numbers is involved.

Many people notice the discrepancy.

Shaking a Fist

The man was not a criminal. He had been driving erratically.

There was something unusual about the man.

The policeman quickly knew that the man was in danger.

A Shooting

Rob was not a police officer, nor was he acting in self-defense. Bill was not a criminal. His murder was in no way justified.

Rob had had no intention of killing Bill. The police were satisfied that someone other than Rob was the murderer.

Their professions are important.

Shooting a Dead Man

The policeman knew that the man was already dead.

He wanted someone else to see what he was doing.

He was not tampering with evidence. He was trying to get information.

The Shoplifter

She does not stop, because she is in danger of being caught.

She steals under a certain guise that enables her to gradually steal larger items.

She is recognized on her regular circuit, but is not known to be a shoplifter.

The Signal

John did not have any special extrasensory or psychic powers.

James received the signal, but not by sight or touch or feel.

John often went out with James for a walk together.

Six-Foot Drop

The tomato fell six feet.

It was a regular tomato.

The man was fast.

The Slow-Car Race

The desert and the full fuel tanks are not important here. What is important is that the last car back wins the race for its owner. The driver raced back in order to win the race.

Slow Drive

There is nothing wrong with the man, the car, the road, or the driving conditions.

This happened under very particular circumstances. At other times he drives at normal speeds.

If he went faster, he would lose something he values.

Small Furniture

They make the furniture for a special kind of house.

The furniture is seen by many but used by very few.

Space Shuttle

This has nothing to do with the materials that the space shuttle is made of, nor with the radio communications.

The direction of the shuttle's flight and the nature of its exhaust are relevant.

Speeding

The police officers would have liked to have booked the man, but they could not. Both officers had given out several other speeding tickets that day, and they were eager to do it again.

The man was not a doctor or a diplomat. He had no good excuse or exemption.

The answer relates to jurisdiction. Although the man had clearly committed an offense, and although a police officer with jurisdiction was present to give out speeding tickets, the man could not be given a ticket.

Spraying the Grass

He wanted the grass to look perfect.

Something was different about the spraying this time.

If he had done this regularly, it would have eventually harmed the grass.

Stand at the Back

There was an emergency and passengers were in danger.

It had nothing to do with how the plane was flying or weight distribution.

The Statue

No ramps, slides, or levers were used. The statue was not tilted or dropped.

The statue was lowered using ropes. The ropes were removed. The statue then settled very slowly onto the base.

Statue of an Insect

The insect had caused a big problem.

The town's prosperity depends on agriculture.

The insect's actions caused a change.

The Stiff Gate

The host was a famous inventor and engineer.

The guests, in pushing open the gate, were performing a useful job for the host.

The Stockbroker

He sent out many predictions, but he was not a good predictor.

Stop/Go

The individuals are not color-blind or disabled in any way.

Their purpose and approach is serious and includes the use of a stopwatch, pencil, and paper.

From time to time the people change one aspect of the vehicle they are driving.

Straight Ahead

It was not done for economic reasons.

The straight miles make no difference to traffic conditions.

The straight miles were designed for use in extreme circumstances.

Strangulation

She was strangled to death with a scarf.

No dancing was involved.

She should not have been in such a hurry.

Suspense

This was a regular occurrence on this particular railway. It allows an essential change to take place.

Although the rail car being lifted so high in the air does shock new passengers, the reason for this action is not difficult for them to gauge.

The Swimmer

There was nothing amiss with the pool, the water, or the ambient conditions. The problem of recognizing the time concerned Sylvia Ester.

She was a well-known swimmer who had won many other events in recognized times. But there was something different about her swim this day.

Talking to Herself

The man was recording something for his archives.

She held a unique distinction.

Teenage Party

The boy and the house gave no clue to the fact that the boy had been drinking.

The place where the gin was kept is relevant.

The father did not like a lot of ice in his gin and tonic.

The Test

Each boy deserved the grade he was given.

There was something unusual about the test.

Jerry was not as diligent as he should have been.

Three Spirals

It appeared as though she was receiving something for pleasure, but for her it was deadly serious.

She was involved in dangerous and illegal activities.

The spirals contained information.

Too Polite

The polite man did not say anything. He simply made a very polite action at an unfortunate time.

He was in a large office, going from one department to another.

The Tower

There were no safety nets, ladders, or scaffolding. If he had jumped from the other side of the building, he would have been killed.

The Trial

The prosecutor had arranged for the announcement of the missing man's "return," knowing full well that it would not happen.

The accused man knew that the missing man could not return.

The Twelve

The twelve people who have achieved this feat were all men. They were not especially rich or influential or exceptionally talented, but they were intensively trained.

The twelve people who have done this all did it within a ten-year period in the 1960s and 1970s.

Two Clocks

They were fully functional clocks that were used to measure time.

The clocks were used only occasionally and never when the man was on his own.

The man had a particular hobby.

Two Men

The death of one man resulted in a benefit to the other.

The man who was happy was not responsible for the other man's death, but he knew exactly when it would happen.

The Unbroken Arm

She was not seeking sympathy or help. Nothing was concealed in the cast.

She was about to do something important.

She knew that the plaster cast would be noticed immediately.

Unclimbed

It is not underwater—it is clearly visible aboveground.

It would be very difficult to climb.

The Unhappy Patient

The doctor took an X-ray.

The patient was warned that "anything found may be used in evidence against you."

Unknown Recognition

The man was physically normal and there was nothing abnormal about his appearance.

I am not related to him, but a relationship is involved.

The Unlucky Bed

All the patients who died were seriously ill, but they were not expected to die.

There is nothing wrong or dangerous about the bed or its location.

No doctors or nurses are involved in the cause of the deaths.

Patients receiving particular treatment are put in this bed.

Up in the Air

It is small.

It does not fly.

Check your assumptions on every word of the puzzle!

The Unsuccessful Robbery

Their timing was very poor.

The bank had had plenty of money at the start of the day.

Vanishing Point

The place the man wanted to go to is well known, but very few people go there.

The man was taken to the famous place and saw what he expected. He later discovered that it had not really been the famous place, but no one had deceived him.

The place is marked, but it is not on land.

The Ventriloquist

The ventriloquist could do much better tricks with one dummy than with his other dummies.

Walking Backward

There was no one else in the house.

The man was not afraid of any danger to himself.

He did not know who had rung the bell.

He ran out the back in order to run around to the front of the house.

Waterless Rivers

This is not a physical place.

It has mountains, but you could walk over them easily.

The cities, forests, mountains, and rivers are real places on planet Earth.

Weak Case

He paid his bail fully and promptly, but paying it incriminated him.

He paid in cash, but it was untraceable.

Well-Meaning

There were several of these creatures in a public place.

They were facing death.

She made a false assumption about the conditions necessary for their survival.

Western Sunrise

No mirrors or reflections are involved. The man saw the celestial sun rise in front of him in the west.

He was on the planet Earth, not in a space rocket, or in space, or at the North or South Pole.

Looking west, the man first saw the sun set, then a little later he saw it slowly rise again.

Window Pain

Both the windows are perfect squares.

Their areas are different.

They look different.

Winning Numbers

If I participate, I will have the same chance as everyone else.

I am in no way prohibited from playing or winning.

The piece of paper has next week's winning lottery numbers on it. It also has last week's winning numbers.

Wiped Out

She worked as a cleaner in a large building.

She cleaned on every floor.

She did much more work than was necessary.

Without Drought

A technique was learned for increasing rainfall.

The Woman in the Ditch

She was an actress.

She wanted to appear shorter than she really was.

Wonder Horse

The horse did not deserve to win.

The weather was relevant.

This horse did not work as hard as the other horses in the race.

The Writer

It was a long process.

Somebody helped him.

He used a part of his body that was not paralyzed.

The Wrong Ball

The ball was clearly visible and accessible.

He did not touch the ball or examine it. He knew it wasn't his immediately upon seeing it.

You Can't Be Too Careful

The pure medicine tastes very bitter.

They do not buy it as a medicine, although it is medicine.

It is effective against malaria.

THE ANSWERS

The Accident
The other car was a hearse, and the passenger was already dead.

Acidic Action
The woman's body was completely dissolved, but she had a plastic tooth that was not soluble in the acid.

Across the River
They walked across; the river was frozen.

Adolf Hitler
This apparently true incident took place during the First World War when Adolf Hitler was a private in the German army. He was wounded and the British soldier thought it would be unchivalrous to kill him.

Adrift in the Ocean
They are in the vicinity of the mouth of the Amazon River. The outflow of river water is so huge that the Atlantic Ocean in that region consists of fresh water for hundreds of miles.

Ageless
The couple had been rock climbing together and they fell. He was rescued, but her body was trapped in a glacier. He was present when her body was finally recovered fifty years later.

Alex Ferguson
Alex Ferguson chews gum incessantly during soccer games. The sale and use of chewing gum are illegal in Singapore.

Alone in a Boat
The two animals were skunks that had been ejected from Noah's Ark because of the stench they were causing.

Ancient Antics
No new species of animal has been domesticated in the last four thousand years. The ancients domesticated dogs, cats, cows, sheep, horses, etc.

Angry Response
The man had said he would be home at 8:00 P.M. He arrived the following morning at 8:02 A.M.

Another Shooting
In this true case, a robber had taken a woman as a hostage after his robbery. When the police tried to free her there was a shoot-out. The hostage was found to have been shot by a police bullet. The court decided that the robber had been guilty of her murder.

Anywhere in the World
The pilot was due to fly from one point to another lying exactly opposite on the surface of the Earth. If we consider the Earth to be a sphere, then there are an infinite number of routes from a point A to a point B diametrically opposite to it. The pilot could set off in any direction and still have the same flight time. It follows that it would be possible to plan a straight course from A to B which would pass over the place where the other man wanted to go.

Assault and Battery
John is a newborn baby. The doctor slaps him to make him cry and use his lungs.

The Auction
The man was bidding for a parrot that was such a good mimic that it bid against him!

Axe Attack
This incident occurred during the French Revolution. The woman had seen her father beheaded at a public execution

by a masked executioner wielding a large axe. The man kept the axe in his bathroom (he had to keep it some-where!). When she saw the axe, the woman knew that the man must have been the executioner who had killed her father.

The Bad Driver
James never drove his car during this period.

Bald Facts
The woman was French and fell in love with a German officer during the German occupation of France. After the liberation, a mob shaved off all her hair and branded her a collaborator.

Bare Bones
The student was pregnant. She had two femurs of her own, two of her unborn baby, and one in her hands.

Barren Patch
Years earlier a troubled airplane had dumped its fuel onto this patch of land.

Biography
The author wrote the biography of Marie Curie, the great French scientist who made many important discoveries concerning radioactivity. She won two Nobel prizes but died of leukemia caused by radiation. The biographer col-lected many of her writings, belongings, and experimental apparatuses to help him write about her. Unfortunately, most of the memorabilia were highly contaminated with radioactivity, and he died later as a result of being exposed to it.

Bombs Away
The plane was already in free-fall.

The Book
The man was the author of the book. On a visit to Tokyo, he recognized the cover design and was delighted to see that it had been translated into Japanese. He was more than happy to buy the book to show to his friends.

The Boss
He fired the new employee on the spot!

Bottled Up
She took home the man's empty champagne bottles after a party. She then left them out with her garbage for collection in order to impress her neighbors.

Bouncing Baby
The baby fell out of a first-floor window.

The Building
It was in medieval times and the man was on the run from a group of angry traders whom he had robbed. He reached a church and claimed sanctuary within it. His pursuers could not arrest him in the church and, if he waited long enough, he could get away.

The Breeze
The man was windsurfing from Cuba to the United States in a desperate attempt to reach freedom.

Brunelleschi's Challenge
Brunelleschi brought the egg firmly down onto the table, thereby cracking and slightly flattening one end. The egg then stood on end. All the other contestants had assumed that the egg must remain unbroken, but this was never a condition.

The Burglary
The couple had given their keys to an honest and

conscientious neighbor. One day a delivery van had arrived. The van driver told the neighbor that he had a chest of drawers ordered by the couple for delivery. The neighbor unlocked the house and carefully watched the van driver and his mate carry the chest of drawers inside. An hour later, the van driver returned and apologized; he had delivered the chest to the wrong house. The neighbor again watched as the chest was removed. Hidden within this piece of furniture was a dwarf. He had, of course, removed all the small valuables he could find during his stay inside the house.

Burnt Wood

Every two years England plays Australia at cricket for the "Ashes." Its name stems from an epitaph published in 1882 following Australia's first victory over England. The article lamented the death of English cricket and stated that its remains would be cremated. The following year the ashes of a burnt cricket stump were presented in an urn to the captain of the English team. The urn has remained ever since at Lord's Cricket Club in London. Each "Ashes" series consists of five or six five-day matches that are fiercely contested and generate a huge following in both countries.

Bus Stop I

While repairing the chair, the man had accidentally stuck his hands to it with superglue. He was waiting for a bus to go to the hospital to have the chair removed from his hands.

Bus Stop II

The road on which the building stands is on a steep hill. The woman prefers to go past the building and walk down the hill, rather than alight earlier and walk up the hill.

Business Rivalry

Cain and Abel were rival train operators involved in the shipping of cattle by rail. When Abel lowered his shipping rates well below cost, Cain dropped out of the rail business and instead bought all the cattle he could find, making a fortune by shipping them to market on Abel's trains.

Bypass

When the bypass was built, a bridge was built over it so that townspeople living nearby, but on the other side of the bypass, could still easily reach the town market. Unfortunately, the bridge over the bypass was not high enough to allow the passage of trucks underneath, so their drivers had to continue using the road through the town.

The Carpet Seller

The cut is made, in feet, as shown below.

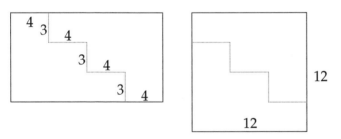

The Cartoonist

He draws cartoons in which small objects are concealed. The drawings are used to test the ability of trainee pilots to detect targets in camouflaged backgrounds.

Cartoon Character

The cartoon character who owes his existence to a misprint in a scientific journal is Popeye. He was invented to encourage children to eat spinach, which was thought to contain large amounts of iron. But this information was based on an error in a scientific journal—the decimal point had been put in the wrong place, making the iron content of spinach appear ten times higher than it actually was.

Cash in Hand
Smith and Jones were travelling on the subway when a gang of muggers came into the car and started to take everyone's money. Smith offered to repay his debt to Jones just before the robbers reached them.

Chimney Problem
The man on the tall chimney had a penknife in his pocket. With this he pried loose a brick from the top layer. He used the brick as a hammer. In this way, he gradually demolished the chimney by knocking out all the bricks and lowered himself to the ground.

Circular Tour
Most people take one stride that is ever so slightly longer than their other stride. Over a period, this results in their walking in a huge circle. Incidentally, most athletes have a right stride longer than their left stride, relating to the fact that they always run clockwise around athletic tracks.

Clean Shaven
Bearded men could be grabbed by the beard in close combat.

The Climber
He hid one boot behind a rock and then hid the other a short distance farther on. He reasoned that, whereas one boot may be found, it was unlikely that the same person would find both boots, and since one boot would be of little or no value it would not be taken.

Complete Garbage
The man was sleeping in a garbage can that was taken to the compactor.

The Courtier
King Alfonso XIII of Spain was completely tone deaf. The man's function was to tell the king when the national anthem was being played, so that he could stand up.

Cross the Gorge
Very light fibers were sent across the gorge attached to a kite. These fibers were then used to pull strings across, which were used to pull ropes across, and so on until heavy cables were stretched across the gorge.

The Cruel King
The king had asked the men to design and build the world's strongest strongroom, where he could safely keep his treasures. Once he was fully satisfied with the workings of the strongroom, he had the men executed so that they could tell no one its secrets.

Dali's Brother
Salvador Dali died at age 7. Nine months later his brother was born and was also named Salvador. It was the younger Salvador Dali who became the famous surrealist painter.

Dance Ban
The dance contest is a limbo dancing competition. The man banned was a dwarf, who had a natural advantage in getting under the low bars.

A Day at the Races
The man was a thief who had made money at the races by picking pockets. After the policeman took down all his details, the man picked the policeman's pocket. The policeman returned to the station with no written record. He didn't remember the details because he didn't think he would need to remember them.

The Deadly Climb
The man who died had been scuba diving in the sea that morning. Ascending to the high altitude so soon gave him an attack of the "bends," where nitrogen dissolved in the bloodstream decompresses and is released as bubbles. It was this that killed him.

Dead Man, Dead Dog
The field was next to a lake. The man had been poaching fish by dynamiting them. He threw a stick of dynamite into the lake. Unfortunately, the dog chased the stick, retrieved it, and carried it to the man, who had run away across the field—but to no avail.

Debugging
If ants gathered around the place where a person had urinated, it was a strong indication that the person had diabetes. The ants were attracted by the sugar in the urine.

Don't Get Up
The woman lives in an apartment building. She hears the phone ringing in the adjacent apartment. She knows that her neighbor, who is a brain surgeon, is out.

A Door Too Large
This one is really a "snip"! The piece he cut off was too small, so he cut another piece off. The "it was too small" refers to the piece he had cut off, not the door.

The Drive
The man was just learning to drive. He did not yet have a license, which would have allowed him to drive on the road, but he could drive on their private drive. The woman, his mother, turned the car around at the road so that he could continue to practice by driving back along their long drive.

88 Too Big
The man was an English tourist in the U.S. He was alone in an apartment when he had a heart attack. He crawled to the phone and dialed the English emergency number, 999, instead of the 911 used in America.

The End of the War
It is recorded that the war ended on a day when there was a total eclipse of the sun. Each of the armies took the eclipse as a sign that the gods were angry with them. Astronomers can date the eclipse very accurately.

The Engineer
The engineer was killed when a large tree fell on him. The dam the engineer went to see had been built by beavers, and a particularly industrious one felled the tree.

Exceptional Gratitude
Bill and Ted were neighbors. Ted kept chickens. Ted's chickens had been wandering through a gap in his fence and pecking around in Bill's garden. They had never laid an egg there. But after Bill thanked Ted for the eggs that his chickens had laid, Ted quickly fixed the fence to stop the chickens from getting out.

Export Drive
Many Japanese exporters relocated their factories to a little Japanese town called Usa. They could honestly stamp on their products MADE IN USA.

Fair Fight
The boxer was a dog that had just won the championship at a dog show.

The Farmer

When the farmer awoke that morning he had seen a rainbow in the sky. It seemed to end in his field. He dug up the field in order to find the pot of gold!

Fill Her Up!

The woman saved carefully and bought her husband the car as a surprise anniversary present. She had it delivered into their driveway and completed the paperwork with the salesman who brought it. Her husband was a cement truck driver. He was jealous and suspicious. He came home unexpectedly, and when he saw the new car in his driveway and his wife talking to a smartly dressed stranger, he assumed the worst. He reversed his truck and dumped his truck's load into the car.

Fingerprint Evidence

When Bundy's apartment was searched, none of his fingerprints were found. This fact was used by the prosecution as evidence of his compulsion to clean fingerprints in all situations—showing his guilt.

Fired for Joining Mensa

Anne works for Mensa in the administration of admission tests. Under Mensa's constitution, no member can be an employee.

500 Times
Hairs on the head. Florence is a brunette, and Washington is a bald man.

Flipping Pages
I was photocopying the book.

The Forger
He was red-green color-blind. The note was colored red. (He had problems with traffic lights as well as paper!)

The Forgery
When the calendar was adjusted in England in 1752, eleven days were skipped. The date on this document was one of the eleven days that never existed!

Free Lunch
The man was a piano tuner who had come to tune the piano in the restaurant. He brought his own tuning fork. The restaurateur repaid the service with a free lunch.

Full Refund
The couple had a little baby with them. They were allowed into the theater on the condition that they leave if the baby cried, with their money refunded. After about 20 minutes, they realized that the movie was terrible, so the mother pinched her baby to make it cry. They left with a refund.

Garbage Nosiness
On our street we put the cans out on the curb for collection every Monday morning. I forgot to put the can out two weeks in a row. Looking in my neighbor's can was the easiest way to confirm that I had missed the collection.

Gas Attack
The unfortunate man was August Jager who had served in the German army in World War I. He was sentenced to ten

years' imprisonment in 1932 for treason. He had deserted in 1915 and been taken by the French just before the Germans launched the first-ever poison gas attack. The French asked him what his gas mask was and he told them. Ironically, it was only in 1930, when the French General Ferry wrote his memoirs, that it was revealed that Jager had told the French about the impending attack. The French ignored the information and took no evasive action. However, the German court found Jager guilty of treason in view of the fact that he had not thrown away his gas mask.

Getting Away with Murder
Many years earlier, the man's wife had faked her own murder and had run off with her lover. The man had been tried for her murder and convicted. He had served a twenty-year sentence. When released, he found her and shot her, but he could not be convicted of the same crime twice.

The Golden Vase
The thief hid in a broom closet after closing time at the museum. He opened the closet door and threw a boomerang which broke the electronic field before returning to him. He quickly grabbed the boomerang and retired to the closet. The guards came running but found everything in order. When they went away, the thief repeated the feat. This happened several times. Eventually, the guards decided that the electronic system was malfunctioning and they switched it off. The thief then sneaked out and replaced the vase with a replica.

The Golfer
Jones was on the wrong green. Two different holes had greens that were fairly close. The two holes lay in a straight line. Jones hit his putt hard in the direction of the other green.

Golf Bag

To deliberately ignite the paper bag would be to interfere with his lie and incur a penalty. So while he pondered the problem he smoked a cigarette. He discarded the cigarette onto the bag and it burned. No penalty was incurred.

Grease

The man's head had been stuck in a railing. A fireman rubbed grease on the captive's head to help free him.

Great Detection

He had written the note on the back of an envelope that had his name and address on the front!

The Great Wall

He was an astronaut standing on the moon—from where the Great Wall of China is visible.

Happy Birthday

The man went to the eye doctor to have an eye test. The doctor looked at his record and noticed that today was his birthday.

Headline News

The editor knew that this trial was the big story of the day, so he had two versions of the newspaper printed—one with the story that Jones was found guilty, and one with Jones found innocent. He then simply distributed the correct version.

Hide-and-Seek

Jackie had a sudden attack of the hiccups. These were so loud and regular that most of the children easily heard her. John, however, was deaf.

High Blood Pressure
Gerald is a giraffe. The average blood pressure of a giraffe is three times that of a human being. This higher pressure is needed to pump the blood up that long neck!

Hole in One
She got a hole in one—but on the wrong green! Driving off the first tee, she holed out on the adjacent, 18th, green.

Homecoming
In this true story, the executive had had shipped back to New York a thirty-foot sailing junk (Chinese boat) that he had bought while in Hong Kong.

Homing Spaniards
Whenever possible, the Spanish explorers took with them a mare who had recently given birth to a foal. They left the foal at their base. The mare would invariably lead them back.

Hosing Down
This incident occurred just before the start of the Monaco Grand Prix race, which is held in the streets of Monte Carlo. Part of the course runs through a tunnel. When it rains outside, the firemen hose down the road in the tunnel in order to make the surface wet. This improves consistency and safety.

Houdini's Challenge
He offered to "make the challenge even more difficult" by being locked inside the safe. He had guessed correctly that the safe was far easier to unlock from the inside than from the outside.

The Impostor
The authorities asked the woman to take a blood test, and she agreed. The real Anastasia was a hemophiliac, who would never have consented to a blood test.

The Investigator
The man had made a claim against his employers for an industrial injury that he claimed had damaged his back so severely that he could no longer bend down. The private investigator had been hired to gain evidence that this was not so. He took photographs of the man bending down to examine his flat tire.

Invisible
The object is an airplane propeller, which rotates so fast that it cannot be seen.

Jam Doughnut
President John F. Kennedy, on his visit to Berlin, tried to express solidarity with the people of the city by saying in German, "Ich bin ein Berliner." Unfortunately, he had been badly advised, since the phrase "ein berliner" in common German use did not mean an inhabitant of Berlin but a jam doughnut.

Job Description
The two men were sitting by the window in the restaurant. As the woman passed, one of the men made sexist remarks to the other man, implying that the woman made her living by immoral means. She stormed into the restaurant and went up to them and said, "Actually, I am a lipreader."

Large and Small
The strong, fit, large people were oarsmen taking instructions from their coxes in preparation for a rowing regatta.

Leadfoot and Gumshoe

The woman is the wife of the chief of police. In order to avoid any impression of favoritism she accepted the ticket and paid the fine.

The Less-Costly Capital

The capital city in question is La Paz, Bolivia. It is the world's highest capital, lying between 10,700 and 13,200 feet (3300 and 4100 meters) above sea level. At this altitude there is less oxygen and fires do not light easily. La Paz has very little need of a fire service, and so saves money.

Light Saving

The sockets were adapted so that bulbs with a left-hand screw were used. Unlike most other bulbs in sockets, they had to be twisted clockwise to be released. When would-be thieves tried to unscrew the bulbs, they were unwittingly tightening them.

Machine Forge

This true story concerns a confidence trickster. He sells the machine to a crook claiming it will generate perfect forgeries. He demonstrates the machine by feeding in green paper. But this green paper is actually genuine $100 bills covered in thick green coloring. The machine simply removes the green coloring.

Man in Tights

The man was Superman. He was lying next to a block of kryptonite, the one thing that could knock him out.

Man Overboard

He fell into the Dead Sea, which lies between Israel and Jordan. The water of the Dead Sea is so salty and dense that anyone in it floats very easily.

The Man Who Got Water
This is a true story from Russia. The man had intended to wash his car, but when he returned he found that it had been stolen.

The Man Who Shot Himself
This is based on an actual case. The men were members of rival gangs. When they met, one pulled a knife and stabbed the other in the stomach, leaving him to die slowly and in agony. The dying man shot himself to curtail the pain. The prosecution proved that the man would have died soon after from his stab wounds. The court found the man who had carried out the knife attack guilty of murder.

Matchless
He was the first child born in Antarctica, and therefore the only person who is known to be the "first born on a continent."

The Millionaire
The man was Walt Disney. A mouse came to nibble the sandwiches and it behaved so comically that Walt put out some food for him every night. The mouse inspired the idea of Mickey Mouse, hence the Disney empire.

Missing Items
The ten-year-old boy has kneecaps, which babies do not have. These develop between the ages of two and five.

The Missing Money
The man had on a different pair of trousers in which he just happened to leave five dollars.

Misunderstood
The instructions given to police dogs are normally in a language not often spoken in the U.S., such as Hungarian or Czech. This is to make it unlikely that any person other than the trained police officers will be able to control the dog.

Motionless
The man was having his portrait taken in the very first days of photography.

Motion Not Passed
Although 35% of the people voted for the referendum motion and 14% against, there were not enough votes overall for a quorum to be reached. It needed 50% of the population to vote in order for the results to be valid. If another 1% had voted against the motion, it would have carried.

Murder
The elderly woman was poisoned by her greedy nephew, who wanted to inherit her fortune. He sent her what looked like a mailer with a fantastic offer for a collector plate which he knew she would want to have. To order the plate, the offer had to be completed, folded and sealed, and sent back without delay. The nephew had put a slow-acting poison on the seal of the mailer. Once his aunt had licked the seal and posted the mailer, there was nothing to connect him to her murder.

A Mysterious Death
The unfortunate man had been hit by a tiny meteor that had penetrated his brain.

No More Bore
Winston Churchill told his butler to go to the door smoking one of Churchill's finest cigars.

The Nonchalant Wife
The woman's husband had committed suicide three years earlier. The cat had knocked over the urn containing his ashes. After she finished her cup of coffee, she swept his remains back into the urn.

Nonconventional
If a nun wants the salt, she asks the nun nearest the salt if she would like the mustard, which is near the first nun. The second nun would reply, "No, but do you want the salt?"

Nonexistent Actors
The movie is *Sleuth*, starring Laurence Olivier and Michael Caine only. If moviegoers were not fooled into thinking that there were other actors involved, it would give the plot away. At one stage Caine leaves and returns in disguise.

No Response
The man had a stutter. The stranger who asked him the question also had a stutter. The man thought that if he answered and stuttered, then the stranger would think that he was being mocked, so the man decided not to answer.

The Nosy Student
Judy hid her letters in her roommate's textbooks, as she knew that was the one place that the roommate would never look.

Noteworthy
A burglar had broken into the woman's house and taken all her savings. In trying to collect the last bill that was stuffed into a jar, he tore it in half. She reported the incident to the police, and then took the half of the bill to her bank. They told her that a man had been in that morning with the matching half!

November 11
When data entry clerks entered customer records onto the computer, the date field had to be completed. However, they often did not have that data, so they simply keyed in 11/11/11.

An Odd Number
In the number 8549176320, the digits are arranged in alphabetical order.

Once Too Often
Voting twice in the same election is electoral fraud—a serious offense.

One Inch Shorter
He was an Air Force jet pilot who had had to eject after a midair collision. The ejector seat threw him out with an enormous acceleration of over one hundred Gs. This acceleration compressed the vertebrae in his back making him an inch shorter. After medical treatment and rest, he recovered to his normal height.

One Mile
When it was originally surveyed, two teams were sent out down the west side of South Dakota. One started from the north and one from the south. They missed! It was easier to put the kink in the border than to redo the survey.

Page 78
The woman was borrowing books for her disabled husband who was confined to the house and a voracious reader. She could not remember which books he had already read, so they had a scheme. Whenever he read a book, or if she brought back a book he did not like, he made a small pencil mark at the bottom of page 78. She could then tell which books to avoid.

Pass Protection

I am describing the end of my journey. My destination is a subway station that is a starting point for many commuters. I bought and used a token at the start of my trip. I simply exit through the turnstiles, passing the lines of commuters coming in.

Pentagon Panic

The missiles are thrown up out of the Earth's atmosphere and then plunge back to Earth. The Earth's rotation, therefore, affects their flight times. Since the Earth rotates from west to east, it follows that a missile will have a shorter flight time from Moscow to New York than vice versa.

Pentagon Puzzle

The Pentagon was built in the 1940s, when the state of Virginia had strict segregation laws requiring that blacks and whites use different bathrooms.

Picture Purchase

The picture was worthless, but it was in a fine frame that he intended to reuse.

The Pilot's Son

The pilot was the boy's mother.

Point-Blank Shot

This true story concerns a striptease dancer who was shot by a jilted boyfriend. Although naked, she was saved by a silicone breast implant that stopped the bullet.

Poisoned

The poison had been put on his false teeth.

Police Visit

The Japanese police first verify that you have a garage or parking space and then give you a permit to buy the car.

Parking space is so scarce in Tokyo that, if you have no parking space, you are not allowed to own a car.

Poor Delivery
The U.S. company stated its required delivery dates in its usual date format, i.e., month/day/year. The European company read the dates as European date format, i.e., day/month/year. So, if the American company asked for a delivery on the 5th day of July 1995, shown as 7/5/95, the European company would deliver the 7/5/95 shipment on the 7th of May!

Poor Equipment
The expensive piece of equipment was a very good watch. The man went to the North Pole, where all the world's time zones meet. Although the minute hand would be correct, the hour hand could be set to any of the time zone hours. There is, in effect, no "correct time" at the North Pole!

Poor Investment
The object is the black box flight recorder from a crashed jetliner.

The Postman
The postman walked around the outside of the wall. The dog followed him, gradually winding its lead around the tree. The effective length of the lead was eventually reduced so much that the dog could no longer reach the path, so the postman delivered the mail.

The Power of Tourism
The place is Niagara Falls, where the water can be diverted from the falls in order to power generators. If the beautiful view of the waterfall was not demanded by the tourists, then much of the water could be channeled through turbines to provide electricity, thus lowering the price.

The Professors
The equation was 9 x 9 = 81 but they were looking at it from different sides of the table. So to one professor it was correct, but to the other it read 18 = 6 x 6, and so was wrong.

Promotion
John was promoted very publicly. He was immediately headhunted by a rival firm, and lured away with a salary he could not resist. The original company wanted to fire him, but that would have been costly. They knew that their rivals were desperate to recruit one of their top people. This way, they got rid of him and saddled their rivals with a dud.

The Quatorzième
He works in a major restaurant and, if called upon, it is his job to join a party of thirteen people in order to bring the number up to fourteen. Thirteen is considered a very unlucky number when dining in Paris.

Radio Broadcast
The noise that deterred the mosquitoes was a frequency too high for the human ear to hear. It drove away mosquitoes, but also, unfortunately, cats and dogs. Listeners complained that their beloved pets fled when the broadcast sound came on.

The Ransom Note
The police were able to get a DNA trace from the saliva on the back of the stamp. This matched the suspect's DNA.

Recovery
The truck had broken down because its brakes had completely failed. The truck driver drove back towing the recovery vehicle. When he needed to slow, he signalled with his hand and the recovery truck driver applied his brakes, thereby slowing both vehicles.

Reentry
The Guinness Book of Records, after 19 years of publication, became the second-best-selling book of all time and therefore got into itself.

Rejected Shoes
The man found that the synthetic shoes generated a buildup of static electricity when he wore them around his carpeted office. He constantly got electric shocks, so he rejected them and went back to his old leather shoes.

Replacing the Leaves
The girl has a fatal disease. She overheard the doctor tell her mother that by the time all the leaves have fallen from the trees she will be dead.

A Riddle
The answer lies in the use of plurals. He did not have eyes, he had one eye. He saw two plums on a tree. He took one and left one, so he did not take "plums" or leave "plums."

Riddle of the Sphinx
The answer is man, who crawls on all fours as a child, walks on two legs as an adult, and uses a walking stick in old age.

Right Off
In this true incident, the car had been struck and destroyed by a large meteorite that the man found lying next to the car. The meteorite was rare and it was bought by a museum for over one million dollars.

Robbery
They started to unload the television sets and carry them back into the warehouse. When the police arrived, the robbers told the police that they were making a late delivery, and they were believed!

The Rock
The man was a deep-sea diver. The sharp rock punctured his suit.

The Runner
In this true incident, the man had been let out of prison for the day in order to enter the marathon. After completing the race, he kept on running to avoid returning to prison.

Russian Racer
The Russian newspaper reported (correctly) that the American car came in next to last while the Russian car came in second.

The Salesman
The house was remote. When the salesman went to plug in the vacuum cleaner, he found that there was no electricity supply in the house.

Scuba Do
The man, who was nearsighted, was on a diving vacation. He had broken his glasses and wore the diving mask, which had prescription lenses, in order to see properly.

The Secretary
She had taken the only key to the office mailbox. She posted it back, so it wound up in the locked mailbox!

Secret Assignment
Ulam went to the university library and examined the library records of all the books borrowed by his students over the previous month. Los Alamos was a common link to nearly all of them.

The Service
The man was a stamp collector. The regular postage

charge for a letter was around thirty cents but, as a special promotion, the post office declared that all letters posted during a certain week need only carry a three-cent stamp. He continued to use the regular stamps on the letters he sent to relatives, friends, and to himself, during that week, knowing that the stamped envelopes would be rare and become valuable to collectors.

Seven Bells
It was originally a mistake, but the shopkeeper found that so many people came into his shop to point out the error that it increased his business.

Shaking a Fist
The man suffered from severe allergic reactions to certain foods. He had inadvertently eaten something that had caused him to have a fit while driving. He veered across the road and came to a stop. He was unable to speak, but waved his hand at the policeman. He was wearing a bracelet indicating his condition. The policeman was therefore able to call for appropriate medical help.

A Shooting
Rob and Bill were actors playing out a scene for a television crime series. Unbeknownst to Rob, someone with a grudge against Bill had substituted real bullets for the blanks that should have been in Rob's gun.

Shooting a Dead Man
This puzzle is based on an incident in the film *The Untouchables*. There had been a shootout at a house and the police had captured a gangster who was refusing to give them the information they wanted. Sean Connery went outside and propped up against the window the body of another gangster, who had died earlier. Pretending the man was alive, he threatened him and then shot him. The prisoner was then convinced that Connery would stop at nothing

to get the information he wanted. The prisoner talked.

The Shoplifter
The shoplifter is a woman who pretends to be pregnant. She has a whole range of false "bellies" under her coat. After nine months, she naturally has to stop.

The Signal
John stood with a dog whistle in his mouth. He gave three low whistles to his pet dog, James, to signal him to come and sit. The frequency of a dog whistle is too high for the human ear to hear but is audible to a dog.

Six-Foot Drop
He caught it just above the ground.

Slow Drive
The man was moving. He was a beekeeper. In his car he had a queen bee. His swarm of bees was flying with the car to follow the queen bee.

The Slow-Car Race
The driver who raced back had jumped into his opponent's car, thus ensuring that his car would arrive back last and he would win.

Small Furniture
The furniture is put into show houses on new housing estates. The smaller furniture makes all the rooms look larger.

Space Shuttle
The exhaust plume of the space shuttle effectively grounds the space shuttle for a considerable part of its initial flight. Therefore, the shuttle could be struck by lightning. A plane is not grounded, so does not conduct lightning.

Speeding

The man sped out of one country and stopped just over the border in another. The first policeman, who had chased him, had no jurisdiction in the second country. The second policeman had jurisdiction but could not arrest or prosecute the man for the speeding offense because it had taken place in another country.

Spraying the Grass

This happened just prior to the 1996 Atlanta Olympics. The groundskeeper sprayed the grass with organic green paint in order to make it look greener for the television audiences.

Stand at the Back

A passenger sitting near the front had smuggled a poisnous snake onto the plane and it had escaped.

The Statue

Blocks of ice were placed on the pedestal so that the ropes on the bottom of the statue fitted between them. The ropes were then withdrawn. As the ice melted, the statue was lowered until it lay firmly on the base.

Statue of an Insect

The insect is the boll weevil, which wreaked havoc with the local cotton crop. As a result, many of the farmers switched to growing peanuts—and became very rich when peanut prices rose.

The Stiff Gate

The host was Thomas Edison, the famous inventor. He explained that everyone who opened his stiff gate pumped ten gallons of water into his rooftop tank!

The Stockbroker

The stockbroker was trying to launch his own business. He bought a mailing list of 4000 wealthy people and sent half of them a prediction that IBM stock would rise the next week. He sent the other half a prediction that IBM would fall. A week later, he chose the 2000 names to whom he had given the correct forecast, and split them into two. Half received a forecast that Exxon would rise. The other 1000 received a forecast that Exxon would fall. Those who received the forecast that came true were again divided, and so on. After doing this six times, the broker was left with 62 people who had all received from him a sequence of six correct forecasts! They, naturally, thought that the stockbroker was a fantastically accurate predictor of market movements.

The stockbroker then called each of them in turn and asked them to move their entire portfolios to his control. They readily agreed, and he had the large portfolio base he needed.

Stop/Go
The people are graduate psychology students conducting an experiment to measure the popularity of various foreign nationalities. In Paris, the students placed German, British, Italian, or Spanish number plates and ID stickers (D, GB, I, E) in turn on the cars. They then drove around, stopping at lights, and measured the length of time it took for French motorists to lean on their horns after the lights changed. They were testing a theory—the shorter the time, the more unpopular the nationality shown on the car!

Straight Ahead
The straight sections were specified so that they could be used as aircraft landing strips in case of war or emergency.

Strangulation
The famous dancer was Isadora Duncan, who was strangled when the long scarf she was wearing caught in the wheel of her sports car.

Suspense
The man was travelling on the Chinese railway system where, for historical reasons, at a certain point the gauge of the rails changes from narrow to wide. Rail cars are lifted bodily twenty feet in the air before being deposited on a frame with wheels of wider track.

The Swimmer
In this actual incident, the officials refused to recognize Sylvia Ester's achievement because she swam in the nude.

Talking to Herself
The woman was eighty-seven. The language she was speaking was dying out and she was the last person to know it. The man was an academic who filmed her to record the language before it was lost forever. (This puzzle is based on the true story of Dr. David Dalby's filming the last woman to speak the African language of Bikya.)

Teenage Party
The father kept his bottle of gin in the freezer, where gin remains liquid even to very low temperatures. The watered-down gin, however, had frozen into a solid block within the bottle.

The Test
The final instruction in the test was to ignore all the previous questions. The teacher had repeatedly told the students to read over the entire exam before beginning. The test was given to see how well the pupils could follow instructions.

Three Spirals
The woman was a spy. She received record albums in the mail. When they were intercepted, they were found to contain music. However, one side had two separate spirals, one inside the other. The inner groove contained the

secret information. She was caught when the authorities noticed that one side of the record lasted only half as long as the other.

Too Polite
The Japanese office worker was in an elevator at work. The doors opened and he saw an important senior executive. He bowed low and his head was caught in the closing elevator doors.

The Tower
The tower was the Leaning Tower of Pisa. The man jumped off on the upper side and landed safely on the floor below.

The Trial
While those in the courtroom watched the door and waited for the missing man to appear, the accused man was being videotaped. When the video was later played for the jury, they could see that the defendant did not even glance towards the door—he knew that the missing man was dead and could not return.

The Twelve
Only twelve men have walked on the surface of the moon.

Two Clocks
The man was an avid chess player. His wife gave him a chess clock. This consists of two identical clocks in one housing. Each clock records the time taken by one player for his moves in a competitive chess game.

Two Men
The man who died was executed in a Malaysian jail for drug smuggling. The other man was in a hospital in Hong Kong awaiting a kidney transplant. He had arranged to buy the kidneys of the executed man.

Vanishing Point
The place was the North Pole. The point is marked on the ice pack over the Arctic Sea. The ice pack drifts, and from time to time the point has to be adjusted. When he returned, the man read that the point marking the North Pole was being relocated.

The Unbroken Arm
The healthy young girl put a cast on her arm before going to take a French oral examination. She figured (correctly) that the examiner would ask her about her injury. She came to the exam prepared with answers about how she broke it.

Unclimbed
The largest-known extinct volcano is Mons Olympus on Mars.

The Unhappy Patient
The man had stolen some diamond rings and swallowed them just before his arrest. The police doctor X-rayed him. He was charged. Then they simply waited for the loot to be recovered.

Unknown Recognition
He was the identical twin brother of someone I knew well. I had heard of him but had never met him before.

The Unlucky Bed
Every Friday morning, a cleaning woman comes to the ward with a vacuum cleaner. The most convenient electrical socket is the one to which the patient's life support machine is connected. She unplugs this for a few minutes while she does her work. The noise of the vacuum cleaner covers the patient's dying gasps. The cleaner reconnects the machine and goes to the next ward. (Although this story was reported as factual in a South African newspaper, it is almost certainly an urban legend.)

The Unsuccessful Robbery
The gang had arrived at the bank shortly after another gang had robbed the bank.

Up in the Air
A dead centipede!

The Ventriloquist
The great ventriloquist was really only an average ventriloquist with a clever partner. He started his act with a standard routine with one or two different dummies. Then he would reach into a large chest and pull out another "dummy," who was really a dwarf that dressed and acted like a dummy. The rapid and humorous dialogue of the two men fooled the audience into believing they were seeing a virtuoso performance in ventriloquism.

Walking Backward
The man walked backward from the front door as he varnished the wooden floor. He left the front door open for ventilation. When someone rang the doorbell, he quickly ran around to the front of the house in order to stop the person from walking inside onto the wet varnish.

Waterless Rivers
A map.

Weak Case
The police charged the man with stealing coins from a vending machine. He was given bail of $400, which he paid for entirely in quarters.

Well-Meaning
The animal rights activist went into a restaurant where there were live lobsters in a tank. She bought them all to liberate them, but freed them into fresh water, where they all died because they can live only in salt water.

Western Sunrise
He was the pilot of the Concorde. It took off shortly after sunset and flew west. It, therefore, caught up with the sun and the pilot saw the sun rise in front of him—in the west.

Window Pain
Initially the square window has sides of about 1.4 feet and an area of 2 square feet. It is as shown below. The second window has sides of 2 feet and an area of 4 square feet.

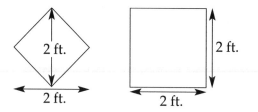

Winning Numbers
One has to choose six numbers from sixty for the lotto jackpot. My piece of paper contains all sixty numbers, so it must contain the winning numbers.

Wiped Out
The woman had been told to clean the elevators in a sky-scraper. She had cleaned the same elevator on each floor!

Without Drought
During the American Civil War it was noticed that the continued firing of cannons caused an increase in rainfall. From this it was learned that firing guns into clouds could cause them to release their water vapor in the form of rain.

The Woman in the Ditch
She was the co-star in a movie and was playing opposite Alan Ladd, who, though a fine actor, was rather short. So as not to be seen towering over her co-star, the woman walked in a specially cut channel alongside Alan Ladd.

Wonder Horse

In this true story, the race consisted of three laps. It was a very misty day. One of the horses stopped at the far side, of course, waited a lap for the other horses to come around, then rejoined the race and won. The jockey later confessed.

The Writer

He winked one eye and thereby indicated to a very dedicated assistant each letter, word, and sentence of the book. He was Jean-Dominique Bauby, the French writer. The book he wrote by blinking, *The Diving Bell and the Butterfly*, was published just before his death in 1996 and became a bestseller.

The Wrong Ball

It had been a cold night and the ball was lying in a small frozen puddle.

You Can't Be Too Careful

The medicine is quinine, which is used to treat malaria and which people buy in tonic water. The British in India suffered badly from malaria until it was discovered that quinine cured and prevented it. Quinine tasted unpleasant, so they put it into carbonated water and created tonic water.

WALLY Test I Answers

Here are the answers to the first WALLY Test. Be prepared to groan!

1. Your feet off the floor.
2. A ditch.
3. Albert. (He deferred to Queen Victoria's wish that no future king be called Albert.)

4. A walk!
5. There are 204 squares of varying sizes on a regular eight-by-eight chessboard.
6. Twelve—the second of January, the second of February, etc.
7. He throws it straight up.
8. Greenland. Australia is a continental landmass.
9. He does not have a door in his pajamas.
10. Five minutes.

Rate your score on the following scale:

Number Correct	Rating
8 to 10	Wally Whiz
6 to 7	Smart Alec
3 to 5	Wally
0 to 2	Ultra-Wally

WALLY Test II Answers

More answers, more groans!

1. ONE NEW WORD.
2. The letter N.
3. Neither—"Seven eights are 56."
4. They threw one cigarette away, thus making the boat a cigarette lighter.
5. 11 seconds. There are 11 intervals as opposed to 5.
6. Whoever the current U.S. president is. His name then was the same as it is today.
7. Tom Hanks and Carl Lewis.
8. No time—you can't have half a hole.
9. He broke out with measles!
10. You should stick it on the package, not on yourself!

Rate your score on the following scale:

Number Correct	Rating
8 to 10	Wally Whiz
6 to 7	Smart Alec
3 to 5	Wally
0 to 2	Ultra-Wally

WALLY Test III Answers

Here are the WALLY test answers:

1. The outside.
2. In the ground.
3. Chap 1.
4. On the head.
5. A leg.
6. Whoa!
7. You would rather the tiger attack the lion.
8. Parents.
9. A dead dog.
10. In the dark.

Rate your score on the following scale:

Number Correct	Rating
8 to 10	Wally Whiz
6 to 7	Smart Alec
3 to 5	Wally
0 to 2	Ultra-Wally

WALLY Test IV Answers

Here are the WALLY test answers:

1.   Concrete floors are very hard to crack!
2.   No time at all—it is already built.
3.   An old ten-dollar bill is worth ten times as much as a new one-dollar bill.
4.   Just one. All the others are anniversaries.
5.   Very large hands.
6.   It is not a problem, since you will never find an elephant with one hand.
7.   Tired.
8.   He sleeps at night.
9.   They were born in Holland.
10.   Fifty. Dividing by a half is the same as multiplying by two.

Now rate your score on the following scale:

Number Correct	Rating
8 to 10	Wally Whiz
6 to 7	Smart Alec
3 to 5	Wally
0 to 2	Ultra-Wally

About the Authors

PAUL SLOANE was born in Scotland and educated at Cambridge University, where he studied engineering. He has worked for many years in the computer industry, primarily in international software marketing. He has always been an avid collector and creator of lateral thinking puzzles. His first book, *Lateral Thinking Puzzlers*, was published by Sterling in 1991, and has gone on to become a bestseller. It has been translated into many languages. Following its success, he established himself as the leading expert in this kind of conundrum. He runs the lateral thinking puzzle forum on the Web at www.books.com and has his own home page. He is an acclaimed speaker on lateral thinking in business. He lives with his wife in Camberley, England. He has three daughters, and tries to keep fit by playing chess, tennis, and golf.

DES MACHALE was born in County Mayo, Ireland, and is Associate Professor of Mathematics at University College in Cork. He and his wife, Anne, have five children.

The author of over forty books, including one on the John Ford cult film *The Quiet Man* and another on George Boole of Boolean algebra fame, Des MacHale has many interests. He has a large collection of crystals, minerals, rocks, and fossils; he was chairman of the International Conference on Humor in 1985; and his hobbies include broadcasting, film, photography, and numismatics. In fact, he is interested in just about everything except wine, jazz, and Demi Moore.

This is the sixth book coauthored by Paul Sloane and Des MacHale, following the success of their other lateral thinking puzzle books, also published by Sterling.

Index

Y

WHAT IS MENSA?

Mensa
The High IQ Society

Mensa is the international society for people with a high IQ. We have more than 100,000 members in over 40 countries worldwide.

The society's aims are:
- to identify and foster human intelligence for the benefit of humanity;
- to encourage research in the nature, characteristics, and uses of intelligence;
- to provide a stimulating intellectual and social environment for its members.

Anyone with an IQ score in the top two percent of the population is eligible to become a member of Mensa—are you the "one in 50" we've been looking for?

Mensa membership offers an excellent range of benefits:
- Networking and social activities nationally and around the world;
- Special Interest Groups (hundreds of chances to pursue your hobbies and interests—from art to zoology!);
- Monthly International Journal, national magazines, and regional newsletters;

- Local meetings—from game challenges to food and drink;
- National and international weekend gatherings and conferences;
- Intellectually stimulating lectures and seminars;
- Access to the worldwide SIGHT network for travelers and hosts.

For more information about Mensa International:
www.mensa.org
Mensa International
15 The Ivories
6–8 Northampton Street
Islington, London N1 2HY
United Kingdom

For more information about American Mensa:
www.us.mensa.org
Telephone: (800) 66-MENSA
American Mensa Ltd.
1229 Corporate Drive West
Arlington, TX 76006-6103 USA

For more information about British Mensa
(UK and Ireland):
www.mensa.org.uk
Telephone: +44 (0) 1902 772771
E-mail: enquiries@mensa.org.uk
British Mensa Ltd.
St. John's House
St. John's Square
Wolverhampton WV2 4AH
United Kingdom

Lateral Thinking Puzzle Books
by Paul Sloane and Des MacHale

Lateral Thinking Puzzlers
Paul Sloane, 1991
0-8069-8227-6

Challenging Lateral Thinking Puzzles
Paul Sloane & Des MacHale, 1993
0-8069-8671-9

Great Lateral Thinking Puzzles
Paul Sloane & Des MacHale, 1994
0-8069-0553-0

Test Your Lateral Thinking IQ
Paul Sloane, 1994
0-8069-0684-7

Improve Your Lateral Thinking: Puzzles to Challenge Your Mind
Paul Sloane & Des MacHale, 1995
0-8069-1374-6

Intriguing Lateral Thinking Puzzles
Paul Sloane & Des MacHale, 1996
0-8069-4252-5

Perplexing Lateral Thinking Puzzles
Paul Sloane & Des MacHale, 1997
0-8069-9769-2

Ingenious Lateral Thinking Puzzles
Paul Sloane & Des MacHale, 1998
0-8069-6259-3

Ask for them wherever books are sold.